THE CULTURE OF HIGHER EDUCATION

A Case Study Approach

James J. Van Patten

University Press of America, Inc.
Lanham • New York • London

Copyright © 1996 by
University Press of America,® Inc.
4720 Boston Way
Lanham, Maryland 20706

3 Henrietta Street
London, WC2E 8LU England

Library of Congress Cataloging-in-Publication Data

Van Patten, James J.
The culture of higher education: a case study approach / James
Vanpatten.
p.   cm.
Includes bibliographical references and index.
1. Education, Higher--United States--Case studies. 2. Education,
Higher--United States--Administration--Case studies. 3. Corporate
culture--United States--Case studies. 4. Affirmative action programs-
-United States--Case studies. I. Title.
LA227.4.V35   1996   378.73--dc20   95-47273 CIP

ISBN 0-7618-0234-7 (cloth: alk: ppr.)

⊖™The paper used in this publication meets the minimum
requirements of American National Standard for information
Sciences—Permanence of Paper for Printed Library Materials,
ANSI Z39.48—1984

Contents

Preface

Several recent books on higher education have explored various aspects of the university culture. This manuscript provides additional insight into our higher education systems through the feelings, attitudes, utterances and actions of those whose work home is in our colleges and universities. These feelings and attitudes are reflected in the cases studies at the end of most of the chapters in the book. The messages contained in the case studies may be helpful in revealing concerns of faculty about their workworld. Through identifying these concerns, efforts can be made to enhance the quality of the work climate of our educational organizations and perhaps lead to a healthier environment.

The public school reform movement that gained impetus from *The Nation at Risk* in 1982 has led to efforts to strengthen educational results. Buzzwords such as performance assessment, outcomes, frameworks, and portfolios are now included in the school personnel lexicon. More attention to specific academic courses within each student's program, longer school days and years, and increased homework assignments are some results of the reform movement. Corporate culture has in many cases been grafted onto the administrative structure of school systems. Efficiency, performance assessment, measurement of output, lean and mean concepts have gained credence in educational policy. In several school systems, privatization experiments have been the result of these trends.

Some new reports suggest that the drive for excellence should not overlook essential needs of non-college-bound, students at-risk, and exceptionally challenged students. Excellence in this view must be redefined to include encouragement of each student to be the best he or she can be with no pre-supposed rigid lockstep college bound achievement levels or preordained test scores.

With nearly two decades of intensive study, research, and widely disseminated reports on essentials of public school reform, the results to date, with occasional exceptions, suggest little if any real change in education achievement levels. In fact, recent education policy reports by Bracey[1] and others indicate many of the reform reports were based on flawed data, misinterpreted analysis, and in some cases preconceived biases.

The reform spotlight has now turned to higher education institutions. The same management models that have been imported into public school systems are now emerging in higher education. Public schools are increasingly discussing the possibility of and experimenting with tying salaries to pupil performance. The same situation is occurring in higher education as assessment, emerging productivity formulas that include student examination scores, retention and recruitment of minorities and women, and graduation rates of athletes, reflect the legislative demands for accountability. Faculty, staff, and administration of higher education institutions are coming under increased scrutiny. This is fed in part by professional associations, parents concerned with increased tuition rates, societal questioning of social institutions, and an anti-incumbency movement within the nation. Privatization is gathering momentum also in America's colleges and universities. To date no public higher education systems have been taken over by private corporations as is the case in the public schools. But bookstores, food services, sanitation, transportation, and the like have been turned over to private corporations in increasing numbers as financial pressures increase and every effort is made to restrain costs.

A confluence of forces is changing the traditional concept of university governance and faculty prerogatives. New non-traditional delivery systems are emerging to serve needs of *placebound students*. Models of collegiality have given way to adversarial relationships as litigation takes center stage in our higher education systems. Various administrative models are being explored to respond to the challenges facing higher education. As we approach the 21st century, one can observe the evolution of specialized administrative offices created to deal with the variety of challenges facing campuses.

Conflict resolution; micromanagement; outsourcing of food services, transportation, bookstores, sanitation and health services; changing student population demographics with students aged 18-24 decreasing in most states represent future trends. In addition, increasing student debt loads (with some students owing some ten to thirty thousand dollars on graduation), increasing cost consciousness of students viewing costs and affordability as well as demanding more from their higher education program are now beginning to face higher education administrators and faculty. Other trends include review of affirmative action, examination of universities student-conduct codes and free speech rights, and increasing fund raising pressures on chief executive officers.

The public often find it difficult to understand what professors do, feeling they are overpaid, teach only a few hours a week, and engage in contemplation which does not fit under the definition of work. There is a constant need to help the public understand the hours of preparation for teaching, the time spent in advising and counseling students, the university and college committee governance activities, the evenings and week-ends spent in publication and research activities.

This book addresses the various forces affecting the culture of higher education. The primary author and the case study contributors wish to keep bias to a minimum, though their own experiences within the academy will tend to affect their interpretation of events within the higher education community. Readers are encouraged to develop their own responses to the various issues presented. They are also encouraged to share their insights with the author.

Wherever possible, case studies are included to identify current issues and dilemmas facing higher education personnel. A chapter is devoted to *Tips for College Teachers: or Faculty Survival in Organizations under Pressure.* With few exceptions case study contributors to this book have served in public colleges and universities from 5-40 years. Any reference to specific individuals is purely accidental. Case studies have been designed to conceal the identity of individuals and institutions. Case studies reflect the interests and concerns of the contributors. As senior faculty can reiterate, the organizational climate in higher education as in all other work environments has ceaseless pressures, frustrations, and challenges. Perceptions about the workplace differ, and those identified in the case studies in this book reflect the experiences of their authors. Our workplaces are never as pleasant as we wish or as deadly as some perceive. As the section on *Tips for College Teachers: or Faculty Survival in Organizations Under Pressure* suggests, some of the morale problems often are due to tunnel vision.

Contributors to this book are: M. Stephen Brown, Dean of Student Affairs, Texas A and M International University, Laredo; Billy F. Cowart, President Emeritus, Western Oregon State College; James T. Bolding, University of Arkansas, Fayetteville; Eugene Buckley, former Director of Institutional Research, University of Arkansas, Fayetteville; Jerry Siegrist, University of Arkansas, Fayetteville; Fred Kierstead, University of Houston, Clearlake; Angela Sewall, University of Arkansas at Little Rock; Deborah Walz, University of Central Arkansas at Conway; and Charlene Hagan, post doctoral student and Amy Marie Charland, doctoral candidate, at the University of Arkansas, Fayetteville. Rhonda H. McDermott, University of Arkansas, Fayetteville deserves appreciation for her careful and thorough editing. George Denny, and Georgia Childers assisted in proofreading. John Townsend and Howard Brill have been involved in the project from its conception. Howard Brill, in the Law College at the University of Arkansas, Fayetteville, pinpoints the increased role of litigation in higher education as the 21st century approaches.

I am especially grateful for the analysis of the manuscript by Dr. Douglas Simpson, Dean of the College of Education at Texas Christian College, Fort Worth. He authored *The Pedagodfathers: The Lords of Education*[2]. Special recognition goes to Robert Sherman, University of Florida, Gainesville and Mario Benitez, University of Texas at Austin, colleagues and friends for nearly four decades who went that extra mile in suggestions and editing.

Many of my colleagues who assisted me in this effort have seen continual transitions in higher education for over a quarter of a century. Organizational continuity and stability in the 1950s were replaced with student protests in the 1960s. The 1970s brought a demand for accountability while the 1980s and 1990s found higher education administrators responding to demands for reform, for increased scrutiny of faculty tenure, sabbaticals and workloads. Many of us can remember a time of more collegiality and fewer adversarial relationships. In the 1950s and 60s there was less pressure for publication, grant acquisition, and research. Being hired, promoted and achieving tenure was less formalized. A reformist mood is currently in vogue in national and state governments that affects the nation's institutions including higher education. In an attempt to respond to calls for more effective government, many state leaders are proposing performance based budgeting. Colleges and universities are increasingly called on to more clearly define faculty workload, explain budget expenditures and demonstrate results for expenditures. The current scene reflects a more complex organizational environment and climate in higher education than in the past. This book explores that environment spotlighting some humorous incidents along the way. As in all large organizations it is vital to maintain a sense of humor to provide needed balance and perspective as bureaucracy often holds center stage.

References:

1.   Bracey, Gerald. W. "Why Can't They Be Like We Were?" *Phi Delta Kappa,* (October 1991): 105-117. "The Third Bracey Report on the

Condition of Public Education. *Phi Delta Kappan,* (October, 1993):105-117.

2. Simpson, Douglas (1994). *The Pedagodfathers: The Lords of Education,* Calgary, Alberta, Canada: Detselig Enterprises Ltd.

Chapter 1

Tips for College Teachers: or Faculty Survival in Organizations Under Pressure

Those entering the academy today face a far different work environment than a decade ago. Opportunities for leisurely pursuit of truth and knowledge, for library research, for in-depth interaction with students are much less than in the past. So often one hears senior faculty yearning for early retirement with the statement "college teaching isn't fun anymore." Others seek the same ends but just want to be left alone in their offices and classes to concentrate on the teaching and writing that they enjoy and find professionally rewarding.

Faculty will not be left alone but will be sought out to engage in a marathon of committee meetings, in revamping course content and syllabi, in being pushed to team with groups of people often with unlike interests to reform, remodel, reformulate whatever has been done in the past. In 210 B.C. Petronius Arbiter, noted the tendency to modify whatever is currently being done within organizations.

> We trained hard, we performed well.... but it seemed that every time we were beginning to form up into teams and become reasonably proficient we would be reorganized. I was to learn later in life that we tend to meet any new situation by reorganizing....and what a wonderful method it can be for creating the illusion of progress while producing confusion, inefficiency, and demoralization.

How the Pros Survive

There are no easy answers. Maintaining good human relations with colleagues and administrators, supporting their change efforts, and working for a positive organizational climate is beneficial. For the majority of senior institutions without collective bargaining, acquisition of a sizable grant allows individuals to escape most of the daily and weekly committee meetings. Going out of town, preferably out of state to present papers at professional meetings, is another escape. Networking with faculty at other institutions for research and interchange of ideas to improve instruction can provide continual renewal.

Those survivors who have been at an institution for more than two decades often find it helpful to speak softly, maintain absolute neutrality, be supportive of new changes, and remain productive. Difficult though it may be, it is seldom good policy to criticize publicly new power centers. When faced with organizational restructuring, survivors often work diligently to become part of as many departmental subdivisions as possible. This is particularly applicable when a faculty member is housed in a deadend program without access to degree programs. Some colleges have more program areas than others, and when that is the case, faculty can have access to masters, specialist, and doctoral programs by serving in more than one subdivision. For those interested in professional growth and development, this is an essential and effective route. Some vested faculty members are jumpers. They are ready to leap on any new bandwagon. If the thrust is toward excellence through bureaucracy, or to requesting change of all course syllabi, or changing the name of the college, the jumpers are ready to leap to whatever emerges on the agenda of the newcomers. Some are observers. These individuals are always ready to take a stance of interest but not action. They are the ones who nod frequently as the new power center takes over, agreeing with all the concepts given. Some are worriers, wondering what new bombshell will fall next. They jump from office to office of trusted colleagues exclaiming in fright "what stupid thing will they do next?" Others are disappearers, preferring to work at home or in the library. The survivors generally are able to maintain a sense of balance in their work, finding release in a variety of outside activities from farming to participation in civic organizations. Survivors need maximum flexibility to function effectively with different management styles. They may have seen ten to fifteen chief executive office, dean and department head changes over their working career. Each management change leads to some modification in office locations, curriculum and mission focus. Survivors need to view each change with support and enthusiasm although they may have seen similar changes result in problematical effectiveness when tried in the past.

Often those who have continuous morale problems are entangled excessively in tunnel vision. These individuals are so engrossed in their narrow field of specialization that they are unable to function effectively within the organization. Such a narrow focus causes individuals to take their worries home, " develop a hardening of the categories" by not engaging in active and reflective listening to other members of the organization or by responding to problems and issues in an absolutist manner. Such a position is detrimental to long term health. Avoiding a sense of ownership in courses taught, membership in departments, or belief that one is indispensable to the organization may be helpful. Having a hobby helps. It provides a sense of wellness so essential to maintain productivity in teaching and writing. When required to attend committee meetings, day dreaming, thinking about an interest area, developing an outline for an article or a book, or planning for future classes is a good method for long term endurance for faculty members. Some survivors create a life time of work through committee meetings. They can expand administrative offices, effectively adding rules, regulations, mandates, hire additional secretarial, graduate assistant, and support staff, and generally harry faculty in many creative ways.

From the faculty perspective, senior and mid-level administrators may use various methods to deal with perceived threats to their power, or faculty who do independent research rather than participate in team projects when the current thrust is toward cooperative efforts, or faculty who have an opportunity for overseas assignments necessitating extended leaves of absence. A college president, on the other hand, may feel a lot like an undertaker in a cemetery. A lot of people are under him but not a lot of people are listening to him. Senior or mid-level administrators may question faculty competence or they may be assigned courses requiring new preparations, or be assigned to off campus satellite centers (often a three to eight hour drive away from their home base) if they openly express disenchantment with organizational goals.

Again, I want to note these measures might not be factors in institutions with collective bargaining, nor is it typical of all organizations. Most college deans and departmental administrators seek to build positive organization climates. One major university formed a committee to enhance the quality of campus life. The end result was a "be nice" campaign which ended shortly after implementation due to complaints from faculty members who felt the campus should be a forum for rigorous debate on controversial issues. Collective negotiation provides some restriction on arbitrary and capricious treatment of faculty.

Whether one is a middle level administrator or a faculty member, there is an increasing tendency for top management to micromanage work. Often assistants to the president or vice chancellor for academic affairs carry modern mobile communication systems, or beepers to reach middle managers. Keeping an eye on every piece of paperwork, overriding the expertise of middle managers, gives the assistants great power. In addition, if anything goes wrong they easily note that it is the fault of middle managers. "I have to retire", "I have to transfer", "I have to get relocated", " I have to return to the faculty", "I cannot stand this any longer" are frequently heard expressions of middle managers. Faculty face the same situation when micromanagers impinge on the traditional faculty roles of advisement, teaching, and research. Excessive numbers of memos, demeaning expertise of faculty members and changing advisement rules at the graduate level serve to expand administration prerogatives. James Boren[1] notes:

> the woof and warp of the fabric of bureaucracy are not the common threads of simplicity, but they are the unending ribbons of red tape that profoundify simplicity and optimize postponement. Red tape, the material that binds a nation into a single, harmonic mass, may ultimately become the final nesting material of our society.

Long-term survivors have seen cycles of change come and go. Many report the most satisfying period of their careers occurred when top level administrators in their colleges were close to retirement. Mellowed, relaxed and collegial, these administrators create a positive organizational climate. They operate on the basis of informed change, not hasty decisions in response to every current fad from within or outside the organization. All of a sudden people feel better, produce more, have better faculty-student, faculty-faculty relations and begin to feel a sense of ownership in their college and university. Faculty strengths are emphasized. Those who love teaching feel free to play to their strengths as do those whose forte is research. Probably one of the reasons for better faculty-student climate during a more relaxed environment is that, as Volkwein and Carbone[2] noted, departments with a balanced orientation toward research and teaching have a favorable impact on students in terms of intellectual growth, disciplinary skills and academic satisfaction. During this period excessive attention to minute details of excessive evaluation is lessened. As Cahn[3] in *Ethics in Academia: Saints and Scholars* notes, the current movement toward computer-generated sheets, rating instructors on a scale of 1-5 results in sending inane data to faculty members with the understanding that these scores will play a significant role in allocation of resources. Cahn finds such a situation demeaning to all involved.

The most difficult time for faculty members is when new administrators work to make an imprint on the organization. They may hold lengthy meetings covering minor items that could be taken care of with a memo. They add additional administrative support staff who review everything that has been done, how it has been done, and why it was done. Everything is up for grabs. Composition of graduate student doctoral committees, programs of study, advisement policy is often reviewed and changed. Undergraduate programs and staffing are frequently changed. Graduate assistants may be assigned to take over the teaching role or senior faculty who have not been teaching undergraduates in many years may be required to teach undergraduates. This oversight management requires new support staff to manage the increased flow of regulations, rules and mandates. Conferences, meetings, retreats are held to analyze and discuss new initiatives. During the "honeymoon" period, when new management can do no wrong, they can distribute extra perks freely generally among new hires. This serves to build a support system. The faculty meetings often reflect the shifting of the sawdust so clearly identified by Thorstein Veblen in The Higher Learning in America[4].

As has abundantly appeared in latter-day practice, these faculties have in such matters proved themselves notable chiefly for futile disputation; which does not give much promise of competent self-direction, on their part, in case they were given a free hand. It is to be recalled....that this latter-day experience of confirmed incompetence has been gathered under the overshadowing presence of a surreptitiously and irresponsibly autocratic executive, vested with power of use and abuse, and served by a corps of adroit parliamentarians and lobbyists, ever at hand to divert the faculty's action from any measure that might have substantial effect. By force of circumstances, chief of which is the executive office, the faculties have become deliberative bodies charged with power to talk. Their serious attention has been taken up with schemes for weighing imponderables and correlating incommensurables, with such a degree of verisimilitude as would keep the statistics and accountancy of the collective administration in countenance, and still leave some play in the joints of the system for the personal relation of teacher and disciple. It is a nice problem in self-deception, chiefly notable for an endless proliferation (p.206).

Some change agents have their own agendas and circumvent, avoid, or eliminate faculty or staff that may be perceived as a threat to new innovative policies. Often there may be a "hidden agenda", such as pushing a particular program to the detriment of others. With the power that money gives to reward and punish, new university administrators can shape the future of institutions. Michael Cohen and James March in *Leadership and Ambiguity* once referred to higher education systems as "organized chaos"[5]. Others have referred to them as "irrational organizations". These terms are used to express the frequent shift in offices, in programs, in staff and faculty, or playing "musical chairs", in which change is invoked for its own sake. It is commonplace to find faculty or administrators retiring and being replaced by from two to four individuals to carry out the same duties these individuals fulfilled for many years. Often for years these retiring individuals' calls for extra help to fulfill their duties fell on deaf ears.

Long term faculty have learned that verbal and written communication from administrators at all levels is to be taken as tentative and provisional. For example, if there are formal and informal rules that there will be no hiring of graduates of the institutions to which they are applying for a job, this can be nullified by a multitude of extenuating circumstances. If there is a job freeze and written communications state that there will be no hiring in a college or department under any circumstances, these statements may merely reflect opinions at a particular time. It may well be that the hiring freeze is a message designed to pressure legislators to increase higher education funding. If there are written and verbal communications indicating there will be no salary increases for faculty or administrators in a given year, notable exceptions may occur due to various unforeseen circumstances. Institutional enhancement funding, acquisition of a large grant or locating overlooked funds are some of the reasons for policy exceptions. "Untouchables" or individuals with special linkages to prominent political figures in the state or to members of the boards of trustees are other reasons for policy exceptions.

Survivors are always aware of the need to be flexible and adjust to changing circumstances. Maintenance staff frequently mow the law outside of classrooms or engage in remodeling work making it difficult for professors to teach and be heard by students. A department or college may have a special event necessitating taking over all classrooms. Faculty then have to search for a place to conduct classes. It may be on the lawn, in a hallway, or wherever the class can gather. Maintenance workers may be placing wall separators in rooms adjoining classrooms, making it difficult for students to hear instructors or visa versa. Faculty members learn to continue their instructional efforts under whatever adverse circumstances come along. Occasionally faculty teaching night courses find all the doors in the building locked. If, as is often the case, no one can be found with keys to open classrooms, other locations need to be found using some class time. Once in a while instructors run over their class time, requiring the next class to gather in hallways until they can gain access to the classroom. In some cases buildings have very thin walls and instructors can hear lectures and discussions from other classes making it difficult to speak loud enough to overcome the noise level. Long term faculty members adjust to all external and internal challenges to their teaching efforts. Meanwhile central administration develops programs and materials for enhancing teaching quality within the institution.

Occasionally colleagues with strong personalities make it difficult for others, particularly when they are working in the same department or program area. Issues of turf expansion and defense may create morale problems. Survivors know how to let go, give up turf, courses and programs, avoid conflicts, and engage in tactful retreat. These turf defense issues are most difficult during a period of interim management at any level within the institution. Over the years these challenges dissipate. An effective operating model is to be supportive of colleagues, build up their achievements and assist them in their goals whenever and however possible.

Cultural Change

Survivors also accept the fact that organizational life need not be just or fair. They learn to accept the fact that new hires receive higher salaries and funds for purchase of computers, software, accessories and other material needed for research. As in business and industry the rationale in higher education for salary differential is the need for entry level competitive salaries in the market place. Survivors get accustomed to changes in organizational goals. Often when they were hired, the job description stressed teaching and service. They were required to teach off campus classes often six to eight hour drives one way from their home college. A more recent tendency within higher education to push research, publication, paper presentation and grant acquisition to the front burner leaves senior faculty in a position of either having to buy their computer equipment out of pocket to engage in newly required research studies or accept minimal if any salary increases during the remainder of their careers. Higher education administrators should work to assure equitable distribution of essentials for research to all faculty regardless of length of service. Efforts can also be made to reward faculty on the basis of their strengths. Some are effective teachers, others may prefer and excel in research. Institutional goals, to the degree possible, can be brought in line with individual goals.

It is helpful in long term survival to avoid the "ostrich" effect in which a faculty member operates in isolation from colleagues. Often a faculty member becomes obsessed with a perceived negative organizational climate and feels he or she is being singled out for heavy workloads or excessive off-campus assignments, or exclusion from prestigious assignments and recognition for contributions to the professional field. However, by communicating with others, one quickly finds that others may feel they are in the same situation. Learning that others feel the same pressures and influences helps individuals cope more effectively with organizational stress.

Many of the deep concerns of faculty and staff could easily be dealt with through a reciprocal information channeling. Far too frequently information systems are "garbage in-garbage out" with trivial items, misinformation or inaccurate memos and messages being sent to faculty. Healthy organizations generally stress quality of the information disseminated. Restricted information channels often lead to hearsay, gossip, and frustration. By the same token, excessive information or/ and gossip is equally detrimental. Inundating faculty with information no matter how minute or trivial leads to dysfunctional organizations. Faculty are equally frustrated when too many organizational, course content and scheduling changes are made at one time. A high quality of communication limited to essentials is helpful in maintaining organizational health. Seeking faculty participation for desired curriculum and program changes may be effective in having all involved buy into new focuses and innovations. This would involve proactive planning by administrators.

As we approach the 21st century, higher education faculty, new and senior, will need to prepare for probable, preferable and possible futures. Thomas S. Kuhn in his *The Structure of Scientific Revolutions*[6] addressed the difficulty of change processes and the need for breakthroughs in perception to achieve new levels of discourse. Kuhn noted that paradigms often act as filters that screen data coming to the scholar's attention. College and university faculty face the same pressures for and resistance to paradigm shifts that confront old beliefs and traditional ways of doing things. The information age is just one challenge to old structures. New generations of faculty challenge the old system and create new horizons of research, dialogue, and inquiry. Higher education institutions will need to provide alternative delivery systems for a more diverse non-traditional population in the future. Faculty and students will need to deal with what John Dewey might have referred to as open-ended, multiple solutions that encourage alternative scenario building for a variety of future possibilities.

Faculty face a time when higher education institutions can no longer do business as usual. As the traditional 18-24- year- old student population declines, and is replaced with full and part time workers many of whom are place bound, higher education institutions will have to be responsive to calls for cost containment and fiscal restraint. Faculty and administration will face a new environment where many students on degree completion owe some $10,000 to $30,000 for their college years. The amount may equal a first year's salary. Parents and students, particularly in large private research universities, who pay the full cost of college tuition may begin to question support for student assistantship for non-tuition paying students.

Most effective organizational changes occur when full faculty participation in planning, design and implementation of new models and paradigm shifts over a sufficient period of time to get the input of everyone in the organization. When everyone buys into the change process, there is a sense of ownership in the shifts.

Long-term institutional survivors have been able to maintain a high degree of flexibility, adaptation to emerging paradigms and willingness to explore new horizons. Particularly important in long term staying power is their ability to maintain an interest and curiosity in realms of new knowledge and research. Although with new concepts that create uncertainty and more work, survivors have learned to be proactive in their thinking, but at the same time balance innovation with keeping the best ideas of the past in order to provide for organizational stability.

Case Studies

Case Study #1
A Faculty Member Who Tuned Out

Professor Jeffers had been at a large state research university in the northwest for over twenty eight years. As the years went by his hearing deteriorated. He eventually acquired a hearing aid. Several of his colleagues noted that whenever he was in a university or college committee meeting, he would mention that he enjoyed turning his hearing aid off. Jeffers seemed to thoroughly enjoy preparing for class by reading some texts, or reading student papers during these meetings. When others would be thoroughly engaged in arguing, debating important issues, Jeffers would seem completely contented and totally disengaged from the often hotly debated issues.

Discussion:

What should his colleagues do? Should they encourage him to turn his hearing aid on? Should they completely ignore this action? What should administrators in his college and department do? Since extensive written memos would be sent to all staff and faculty covering all items of the meetings, should he be totally left alone? If Jeffers were not put on any more college and university committees, would he be rewarded for dereliction of the duty of participating in the governance process?

Case Study #2
Responding to the Grapevine

Dean Vocal, managed a midwestern college with over 5,000 students, graduate and undergraduate. He had served in administration at all levels of the educational system and believed firmly in an information network. When he was first hired, Dean Vocal would ask selected faculty members to report to him when there was something he should know. One day he approached Professors Smith and Jones two untenured recent faculty hires. " I have been hearing rumors that you have been badmouthing me and my administrative style", he said. " Just remember when the eagle ---, he will ---- on those who support me."

Discussion:

How would you as a faculty member respond to this interchange? What administrative style was in operation? Would you feel intimidated by the deans reaction to his information channels?

Case Study #3
A Carpet Is No Small Matter

Mr. John Smith, Superintendent of the Physical Plant
Dr. Joe Phone, Academic Vice President
Dear Administrators:
My chairman has delivered your message: **No Rugs.** My carpet stays where it is. Your prohibition comes many months too late to make other than unhappy those (few? Many? I know not) who have already planned to use some type of floor covering, be it throw-rug or otherwise, and be it for color, comfort, or only companionship. Mine went into my office 627 after the first full day I worked there, resulting in such pangs in my bum knee that I didn't sleep too much that night.

I can hear some of the others now: "Why is it that a mere secretary in the !!*?!! Administration Palace gets free carpeting, whilst I, who as a Full (or half-full, or whatnot) Professor, can't have one even if I buy it myself? How is it that some noodnik Secretary is more important than a Prof?" But that's not my style; and besides, I know how mere a Prof is, and that the degree of mereness of a Secretary depends on who the cat is that she secretaries for.

You might hear me agree with another: "Here I am, out $X9.98 for a rug I can't use anyplace else, and now can't use here. If I'd known this three weeks ago, I could've saved myself $X9.98." My own carpet is a thoughtful Christmas present from my wife, who paid for it and over whose dead body you can haul it away, and to whom I refer you for any further discussion of this $ point. But no matter. While all the above is real enough, including the fact that your concrete floors hurt my legs, the State objection is that the University can't afford to buy and man a bunch of additional vacuum cleaners. I know that; I've long known it; you discussed the points some years since at a meeting. Nor are we alone. I have colleagues at other universities whose maintenance limitations are similar to ours--though the colleagues' privileges to seem to differ somewhat.

As it turns out, I have my Very Own Vacuum Cleaner, provided me for use in our old Science Lab in our Old Symth Hall. Free gratis. No charge, for 5 years. Your people don't need to clean my carpet at all, because I had planned to man my cleaner myself, knowing you couldn't---even though I think your budget ought to be increased enough so you can. All I need is for somebody to swipe off the uncarpeted part of 627 and dump out the wastebasket. In view of all which, you don't have any objection at all to the carpet in 627. **It stays.**   Sincerely, O.N. Bushnote, Mere prof.

cc: Academic Vice President Phone, Dr. Moot, Dr. Hope and John Smith.

Discussion:

How would you respond to Professor Bushnote's letter? What observations could you make regarding the attachment to his office and its trappings and the possible changes necessary in space utilization within an institution. Discuss the differing perceptions of administrators and faculty about office ownership?

References:

1.   Boren, James H. (1982). *Fuzzify*, McLean, Virginia: EPM Publishers.
2.   Volkwein, J. Fredericks and Carbone, David A. (1994). "The Impact of Departmental Research and Teaching Climates on Undergraduate Growth and Satisfaction", *Journal of Higher Education,* March, v 65, n2: 147-167.
3.   Cahn, Stephen, (1993). *Ethics in Academia: Saints and Scholars*, Lanham, Maryland: Rowman and Littlefield: 41-42.
4.   Veblen, Thorstein (1946). *The Higher Learning In America.* New York: Hill and Wang: 206 (Originally published in 1918).
5.   Cohen, Michael and March, James (1974). *Leadership and Ambiguity.* New York: McGraw-Hill. Also see Cohen, M.D.; March, J.G. and Olsen, J.P. "A Garbage Can Model of Organizational Choice", *Administrative Science Quarterly* 17, 1974:1-25.
6.   Kuhn, Thomas (1970). *The Structure of Scientific Revolutions,* Chicago: University of Chicago Press.

Chapter 2

Challenges and Issues Facing Higher Education

The spotlight for reform has now turned to the 3,000 higher education institutions staffed with more than 800,000 faculty members in the United States. Calls for reform from *The Association for the Study of Higher Education, The Carnegie Commission,* and a number of other organizations are seeking an examination of how faculty time is spent. Parents, state legislatures, students, community and business groups have added their voices to requests for higher education reform. Mary Jordan in "Respect is Dwindling in the Hallowed Halls",[1] notes that recent congressional hearings and books describing college professors refer to lazy, overpaid and irrelevant faculty. She found them criticized for being too attuned to political considerations, too wasteful of government dollars, too fond of coeds! Jordon cited James E. Perley, president-elect of the American Association of University Professors, as well as the Carnegie Commission's survey noting that respect for academics is eroding. Complaints about college professors include grade inflation, tenure, and ever-escalating tuition. The tendency is to blame tuition increases on the faculty while ignoring increasing administrative costs. Faculty members noted that their university administration pressures them to get grants and publish at the expense of their teaching. Jordon referred to an AAUP spokeswoman, Iris Molotsky, who said it used to be that faculty and administration were two sides of the same coin, (many administrators came from a faculty background) while currently more university presidents are coming from business backgrounds and have little in common with the faculty. Thus, it is clear that the nation's 800,000 university professors as well as the higher education institutions in which they work will be getting an ever-closer look from escalating criticism[2]. Probably a good portion of the criticism is due to the escalating cost of an education.

The response to these voices for reform has too often reflected the mechanistic, reductionists' theories so popular in the early 1900s when Frederick Taylor's *Scientific Management* was introduced. Then, as now, a business/industry mentality is affecting higher education. Layers of inspectors review massive amounts of paperwork--student evaluations of faculty, faculty evaluations of staff, faculty evaluations of other faculty, faculty evaluation of administrators, administrators' evaluations of faculty, administrators' evaluations of staff, administrators' reviews of faculty evaluations of other faculty, administrators' ever-changing formats for evaluations of faculty often based on various committee and commission reports on the subject. Besides the university-wide evaluations, college and departmental committees have gotten into the act. College and university administrators often mandate multiple forms of evaluation. This philosophy is based on Taylor's view that individuals are inherently lazy goldbrickers who need layers of management and supervision to assure maximum productivity and efficiency. Under Taylor's system, time and motion studies were utilized to insure that every individual movement and action added to factory line production in shops. Current evaluation systems in higher education, with adjustments in language and to meet the differences in labor composition, reflect this scientific management view. Accordingly higher education management systems modeled on business and industry models, stress marketplace terminology. Consumers, competition, reengineering, mission statements, strategic planning are terms currently stressed in higher education. These terms tend to replace the historical **Ideal of the University** where the leisurely, reflective, unhindered and scholarly search for truth and knowledge was considered the essence of higher education. Robert Paul Wolff[3] addressed this ideal when he wrote that the fundamental purpose of this community (the university) is the preservation and advancement of learning and the pursuit of truth in an atmosphere of freedom and mutual respect, in which the intellectual freedoms of teaching, expression, research, and debate are guaranteed absolutely.

Professionalism within higher education requires calling attention to anti-intellectualism in theory and practice under whatever guise it is practiced. Excessive quantification of performance and a philosophy of breaking wholes into parts (reductionism) imposes factors detrimental to professional growth and development. Patrick Dolan[4], in his 1976 *The Ranking Game,* wrote about the *American Council on Education* evaluation studies ranking colleges and universities. He suggested that these studies were misleading, deliberately creating the impression that evaluation has risen to a newer, quantifiable level, appearing to be something that it is not. Dolan surveyed faculty members in various disciplines in various universities throughout the United States noting their opinions about the arrogance of ranking games in higher education.

As long-term faculty members can attest, such exponential explosions of bureaucracy, an increasing number of annual statistical evaluation measures, has not led to instructional improvement or to positive organizational climates, but on the contrary has actually been ineffective and demoralizing to professional educators across academic disciplines. Each new administrative position requires self justification. By issuing reports, mandates, and decrees, the workload demands additional support staff. Bureaucracy feeds on itself and increases exponentially. In some areas, there is increased employee turnover, decreased institutional loyalty, and a general angst about lack of an anchor. Mixed messages, uncertainty about institutional, college, and departmental goals require a rethinking of ethics and professionalism in institutional management.

Far too often the purpose of the university as a center for learning and knowledge is secondary to the bureaucratic demands for ceaseless expansion of paperwork. This is not to imply that administrative policy making is not needed in larger higher education institutions, but rather to identify excesses that diminish the essential qualities of a nurturing environment in which faculty, students and staff can grow and learn.

The history of higher education reveals profiles of great university presidents who defended academic freedom, professionalism in academic fields, and the ethics of informing the public of the unique, special role of higher education institutions in society. In recent years, legislative mandates have impinged on the functioning of the university. Too frequently higher education leaders pass along to staff and faculty legislative mandates that are detrimental to the historical **Ideal of the University.** This reflects less on institutional managers than on the power of cycles of the business community's philosophy currently espousing performance assessment, efficiency, downsizing, competing effectively in the market places, serving clients, and a multitude of forms of accountability. As Oliver P. Kolstoe points out in *College Professoring*[5], those who make up boards of trustees and legislative budget committees have less knowledge of the entire two thousand years of academic tradition than those who pursue social reform or nurture for their offspring.

Since most of these officials have achieved their visibility through channels of business or finance, they tend to view universities in terms of debits and credits (p. 132.) The business model is being adhered to in 1996 as surely as in 1918 when Thorstein Veblen wrote *The Higher Learning In America*[6] in which he suggested that the model of ambiguity and evasions (of applying the business model to higher education while pretending to have faculty input) has reached such settled forms and is so well understood that it no longer implies an appreciable strain on the executive's veracity or his or her diplomatic skill. Faculty input, he continues, really belongs under the category of legal fiction, rather than that of effectual prevarication. He notes:

> It devolves, properly, on the clerical force, and especially on those chiefs of clerical bureau called "deans," together with the many committees-for-the-sifting-of-sawdust into which the faculty of a well-administered university is organized. These committees being, in effect if not in intention, designed chiefly to keep the faculty talking while the bureaucratic machine goes on its way under the guidance of the executive and his personal counselors and lieutenants. These matters, then, are also well understood, standardized, and accepted, and no longer require a vigilant personal surveillance from the side of the executive. (185-186)

The ethical, legal and professional responsibilities of higher education personnel ought to be addressed in an attempt to rediscover civility and human decency within our institutions. Neither the mechanistic management theories of the 1920s, nor the policy goals involved in current efficiency theories of management suffice to deal with the needs of our 21st century society. Buzzwords such as downsize, accountability, performance assessment, competitive reassessment, management by objectives all lead to forms of harassment of faculty and staff by inundating them with increased demands for reams of files, reports, committee membership, committee progress reports, etc., and reduce the time available for carrying out the fundamental mission of higher education institutions. Higher education institutions are unique in their role and function as a center for exchange of ideas, for dialogue, disagreement, and dealing with controversial issues essential for an open society. Managers and administrators of these institutions have a moral and ethical obligation to inform political, social, and economic policymakers about the uniqueness of higher education institutions within society. No one points this out more clearly than John Brubacher in the concluding chapter in his *On the Philosophy of Higher Education,* entitled "The University as a Church". Brubacher and John Dewey would concur that a college and university where all races, colors, creeds, genders and ages gather to address problems of society and academics fulfills a religious sense of shared values through dialogue and critical inquiry.

There is increased attention today on the importance of ethical and moral considerations in higher education. Swazey, Louise, and Anderson[7], in *The Ethical Training of Graduate Students,* note the importance for faculty and students to deal with ethical issues within higher education institutions. Faculty members as well as students need to rediscover ethical standards within their academic disciplines.

We can put people power to work by rediscovering the value, worth and dignity of ordinary individuals who with a positive, supportive, enhancing organizational climate can do extraordinary things.

The Law, Ethics and Professionalism

Banks McDonnell, in *Ethical Conduct and The Professional's Dilemma*[8], finds that the average professional is a typical human being, a bundle of contradictions, containing within himself or herself the capacity for genuinely virtuous and altruistic activity, as well as mean, selfish, and greedy activity. He relates the example of Abe Fortas, a noted Supreme Court Justice and successful lawyer who did extensive *pro bono* or charity work throughout his life. He represented Owen Lattimore at the Joseph McCarthy hearings and defending Monte Durham, established the Durham rule for insanity defense. Further time and expertise donation was his representation of Clarence Earl Gideon in Gideon v. Wainwright (1963), which gave us the protection that every criminal defendant is entitled to legal counsel whether or not he or she can afford it. Yet for all this charity work, for all his fame as a lawyer, he was forced to resign from the Supreme Court for improperly accepting compensation from a potential litigant who may have come before him when he was a justice, raising serious questions of conflict of interest in violation of the Code of Judicial Ethics.

All professions face ethical dilemmas. Higher education personnel are not immune. The pressures for acquisition of grants in major research universities has led to unfortunate unethical short cuts as some faculty have now been found to falsify data to expedite their research.

For the last forty years, education litigation has been increasing in state and federal courts due to expanding social consciousness as we seek to provide more access and opportunity for education at all levels for individuals from all classes, cultures, and ethnic backgrounds. Litigation is particularly challenging now as more and more individuals take their claims to the courts, especially when deep pockets are available targets. As noted in Gose's *Lawsuit 'Feeding Frenzy'*[9] the legacy of *in loco parentis*, the once pervasive legal theory that colleges have responsibilities and rights similar to those of a parent, persists. Gose finds that the potential cost of college and university litigation may lead to universities' trying to micromanage student activities because of fear of liabilities. There are, however, limits to restraints that can be placed on students in the 1990s. It is important to connect the law to the ethics, professionalism, and responsibilities of higher education personnel.

Ethics

Ethics concerns general principles of conduct that people should follow in theory and practice. Higher education administration, faculty, and staff should act so as to do no harm, to deliberate within their areas of expertise and competency, and to be committed to the highest ideals of professionalism. With increasingly complex organizations reflecting the competitive pressures of a business oriented society, it is difficult to adhere to a set of general principles of conduct.

Benjamin Barber, in *An Aristocracy of Everyone: The Politics of Education and the Future of America*[10], notes that while Harvard requires all students to take a course in moral reasoning, well intentioned faculty seem to have forgotten John Dewey's caution:

Moral education in school is practically hopeless when we set up the development of character as a supreme end, and at the same time treat the acquiring of knowledge and the development of understanding, which of necessity occupy the chief part of school time, as having nothing to do with character. On such a basis, moral education is inevitably reduced to some kind of catechetical instruction ...lessons "about morals" (that) signify as a matter of course what other people think about virtues and duties[11].

Ethics and Professionalism

The ancient Greeks addressed the issues of virtue and character building. Socrates spoke of the love of wisdom as reciprocal love of knowledge, respect for others, developing social codes of honor, and active, reflective listening to the responses of students as members of the larger society. Socrates, Plato and Aristotle identified marks of a moral act as a conscious, consistent behavior trait, as acting with a commitment to a higher moral law---that of duty.

Some of the Athenian codes of honor represented the moral and ethical focus of the time and contained such statements as "I will leave my country not less but greater than I found it. I will fight, whether alone, or in defense with my fellows to protect and preserve public property and obey the laws made by the magistrates."

Democracy, a pluralistic society, and education are the same. To protect and preserve our higher education institutions from anti-intellectual attacks under whatever guise they come, we need to do our best to defend academic freedom. For as Jefferson argued, the college must free men from superstition, not inoculate them with it. Jefferson would have his university diffuse and advance knowledge[12].

Herring[13] and Cahn[14] explore tenure, academic values, governance, arbitration, and academic freedom in their study of professionalism in higher education. They note the importance of continual reexamination of the rights and responsibilities of higher education faculty and administration. Both authors find a discrepancy between theory and practice in education and identify the need to improve ethical understandings and considerations. Their message points out the importance of faculty keeping up to date in their subject matter, growing professionally, being reviewed continuously with or without tenure, and meeting all contractual obligations in the field of scholarship, governance, and research. A study of the culture in higher education reveals that there are a growing number of external and internal pressures confronting all populaces in the college and university. All academic disciplines face these challenges, but colleges of education are particularly buffeted by public opinion changes. The challenge for professionals is to balance demands for innovation with stability essential to all organizations.

In assuring faculty fulfillment of contractual responsibilities and duties, efforts have been made through the years to evaluate performance. There are no easy answers to evaluating faculty teaching performance, either today or in 1971, when Kenneth E. Eble[15], wrote *The Recognition and Evaluation of Teaching*. Eble identified the case for a more effective means of evaluation for a committee of the American Association of University Professors and the Association of American Colleges:

> The inadequacies of our present procedures for evaluating and recognizing teacher effectiveness are most apparent where decisions are being made about retention, promotion, and tenure. ...In thousands of instances each year. ...decisions [are] made on the basis of extremely tenuous information about teaching ability; a limited amount of student response, usually informal, undiscriminated, and distorted by successive reports, judgments by deans, chairmen or colleagues deriving from social conversations and corridor exchanges, and guesses about classroom effectiveness based on the faculty member's performance of quite different institutional duties (p. 16).

In 1971 when Eble's work was published, some pros and cons of student evaluation of the instructor were set forth:

Pros:
1. Student evaluation increases the chances that excellence in teaching will be recognized and rewarded.
2. Student evaluation encourages participation between student and teacher, especially helpful in large schools.
3. Student evaluation provides the only direct and extensive information about a faculty member's teaching.
4. An institution may be stimulated by student evaluation of teaching to consider its overall goals and objectives.
5. The support of student evaluation is a tangible sign that faculty and administration recognize the importance of student involvement in shaping the institution's goals and practices.

Cons:
1. Student evaluation does little good and some particular harm.
2. Student evaluation may arouse an unhealthy competition among faculty members.
3. Evaluation systems move toward harmful formalization, mechanization, rigidity.
4. Student opinion questionnaires furnish inadequate or misleading information about teachers and teaching.

5. The effect of student evaluation is a short term one connected with the novelty of procedure.
6. Students by themselves will not be able to sustain a high level of evaluation procedures over a period of time (p. 17-18).

Some twenty-three years after the Eble study, with more sophisticated evaluation forms required of all higher education faculty, Cahn[16] notes that computer-generated spread sheets distributed to faculty members each semester results in sending inane data to faculty members with the understanding that their scores will play a significant role in the consideration of their reappointment, promotion, or tenure and is demeaning to all involved (p. 42).

Administrator's Point of View

When faced with the issue of justifying an increasing number of administrators, the response is likely to be that faculty are not in their offices enough to advise students, do not attend governance meetings, or fulfill their institutional duties. Many administrators find that most of the student advising from freshman through the doctorate level is done by departmental secretaries. In addition as noted by Steve Sticklow in "Chief Prerequisite for College President's Job: Stamina",[17] many college presidents spend long hours in fund raising. He notes examples of the challenge of college administration. Judith Rodin, President of the University of Pennsylvania, has a schedule booked solid over six months in advance. She must attend committee meetings, staff meetings, receptions, football games and alumni events--typically a fourteen hour day. On top of this are memberships on boards of the local chamber of commerce and civic group involvement. Dr. Neil Rudenstine, President of Harvard, had to take a medical leave of absence due to being overwhelmed by a job requiring him to raise almost $1 million a day. He has returned to his position seeking to place his workday in better perspective. Many college presidents face severe funding problems which often require institutions to downsize. According to the American Council on Education, most college presidents are finding less and less satisfaction in their job and stay fewer than seven years. Fund raising makes college presidents and others including deans, seem more like salesmen and politicians than scholarly figures. But Stecklow notes that there also is a good side to the administrative position. A recent survey by the *Chronicle of Higher Education* found that in the private college sector some 147 presidents earned at least $175,000 a year with added perks ranging from housing to the best seats at athletic and cultural events.

University presidents are lighting rods for dissatisfaction from a multitude of constituencies including faculty, students, alumni, administrators, and trustees all vying for their particular interests. Pressures on college presidents noted by Stecklow are that they are a lightning rod for any campus dissatisfaction. Dr. Rudenstine was shaken by an angry faculty upset over health care and pension cuts that were allegedly made without consultation with the faculty. Rudenstine feels that faculty lost confidence in him. University and college presidents are often between boards of trustees and faculty and have to implement controversial policies set forth by the board of trustees. In addition, every faculty member hosting a large group, counts on the university president attending his particular conference. Stretching the challenge even farther is the constant demand for dealing with minutiae such as maintaining campus facilities and dealing with rising utility costs[17]. Meanwhile as Brimelow[18] points out, business and industry may organize their own training centers. He refers to Sir Douglas Hague's 1991 pamphlet *Beyond Universities: A New Republic of the Intellect,* published by the London's Institute of Economic Affairs. Hague finds that universities have lost their intellectual monopoly and that individuals outside the universities will be able to innovate with more success, since they are unrestricted by academic custom and tradition. Hague believes technology will revolutionize teaching, and universities are not prepared for the challenge of needed change.

Case Studies

Case # 1
A Case of Plagiarism

Professor Jones had taught for over fourteen years at a major west coast university. He had one of the best publication and teaching records at the university. Each year he had received the highest merit salary increase in his department and college. Jones was well respected in his professional field and had received numerous awards for his contributions. Helen Smith, one of his students had reported Jones to his department head for using her work without giving her credit, several times through the years. Nothing was ever done about her concerns. Late in the spring semester one year, Helen reported Jones to the university academic vice president and chancellor for plagiarism of her work. Not long after this spring report, Professor Jones was dismissed from his university position. Jones insisted the research was his own and that he encouraged the student to expand on the topic. He had tenure and other than this single case, had an exemplary teaching-research-service record.

Discussion:

Should Jones have been dismissed? Should the department head have acted sooner to correct the situation? Jones had a faculty-administrative committee review the evidence in the case. Their recommendation was for dismissal. How should university administrators handle cases of plagiarism? Do you think pressure for publication may lead to such an unethical act?

Case Study #2
A Case of Gratitude for a Job Well Done

Congressman Ted Sampson had served his District in the Northwestern United States well. He had been in the House of Representatives for over 20 years and was able to bring several major projects to a Central State University. Through federal funds the university was able to expand from a community college to a four year institution and later added master's and specialist's degree programs together with a joint doctoral program with the state's research university. On retiring from the Congress, Ted Sampson was given a distinguished university professorship with tenure and a salary of $96,000 by board of trustees action. The average faculty salary for full professors was $47,000 and $57,000 for distinguished university professorship. Ted Sampson did not have a doctorate although he had two master's degrees and over 120 graduate hours beyond the master's in a variety of fields.

Discussion:

Although there were no faculty complaints over the appointment of Congressman Ted Sampson, what ethical concerns might be expressed in regard to the university board of trustees action? Should universities be a repository for individuals who have represented Congressional Districts? Does the university benefit from such largess? Discuss the multiplier effects of such appointments.

Case Study #3
Fatal Attraction

George Hangover, a tenured professor with over 25 years of excellence in teaching at a major state university, became engaged in a case of mutual attraction with a matriculating graduate student who was one of his former students. Cathy Jergen had a rocky marriage and was in therapy to deal with the problem. George and Cathy's relationship rapidly evolved into a case of torrid romance. After reports of sexual activity on Professor Hangover's desk in his university office, the department head had a conference with George. Dr. Bill Wellness told Professor Hangover to keep his romances off campus and cease any further relationship with Cathy on campus. Dr. Wellness knew Cathy Jergen was in therapy and told Hangover that he was in a dangerous relationship. Due to the fact Hangover and Wellness were long time friends and colleagues, efforts were made to settle the situation without reverting to immediate dismissal. Cathy's husband eventually brought a case of alienation of affection against Professor Hangover.

Discussion:

Although sexual harassment cases are increasing in higher education, and written policies are widely disseminated, relationships between consenting adults is subject to varying interpretations. Discuss the ethics of relationships between consenting graduate students and faculty members. Discuss the legal liability of universities for actions of faculty members such as Professor Hangover. The department head wanted to deal with the issue without going further in the chain of command. How would you have handled the situation? Although in this situation, the case was settled out of court, how can administrators deal with the ethical issues involved in faculty-graduate student consenting relationships?

Case #4
A Reward for A Winning Record

Coach Ted Winner had served his northeastern research university well for over 30 years. He had a record of winning 70% of the football games over his tenure at northeastern. Coach Winner had brought great recognition to the university. Coach Ted's winning ways had brought increased funds to the university endowment fund every year. He was recognized nationwide for his athletic prowess and was loved by football fans in his state. When he announced his retirement, the board of trustees immediately gave him a distinguished full professorship with tenure in an academic area of his choice.

Although he could make a major contribution to students with his wide experience in athletics, Coach Ted had only a bachelor's degree in physical education. The department head and the dean of the college in which he chose to be located, provided opportunities for the former coach to serve the university as a motivator, student recruiter and researcher. He always was on the podium giving speeches when fund raising drives were under way.

Discussion:

Discuss the ethics of providing opportunities in academic departments for long time contributors to the university. Is it ethical to fund teaching, research, and distinguished professorships for individuals who have made significant contributions to a university regardless of academic credentials?

Case #5
Maintaining Recognition in an Era of Downsizing

President James Ratherford was faced with a major funding crisis in his university: The Northeastern University, with a historical record of being one of the nation's premier institutions, had to cut expenditures at an early date. Slogans such as retrenchment, recycling and reallocation of resources became campus wide. The state legislature with a dearth of funds sought to find a solution to the problem and asked each university president to find areas for cutbacks or elimination. Ratherford immediately ordered each college dean to direct department heads to come up with a plan for cutbacks in faculty and staff positions, to prepare for possible funding cuts of 5, 10, 15, 20 and 25 percent. Due to a decentralized decision making process which had developed over the years at the university, cutback recommendations were made in the various operating academic units. Public hearings were held to gain the views of all university populations. Faculty members within each college went through the agonizing self examination about which programs to cut back or eliminate. All university faculty meetings were held, with some faculty members calling for shared poverty to save jobs and others wanting to put what university money was available behind younger faculty members in promising growth areas with federal grant possibilities such as the sciences. In the midst of this agonizing effort to downsize, President Ratherford with the support of the board of trustees, offered top salaries exceeding $120,000 plus perks to recognized scholars in their respective fields. The rationale for hiring internationally renowned scholars was to maintain the historic prestige of the university.

Discussion:

As a member of the board of trustees, how would you respond to the hiring of recognized scholars during a period of economic downturn? Is it ethical to dismiss faculty, staff and cut back student support services, while at the same time expend scarce funds to hire top flight scholars? Discuss the pros and cons of such decision making. Discuss the issue of downsizing from the various perspectives of faculty, administration, staff, trustees and students.

References

1.   Jordan, Mary (June 20, 1994). " Respect Is Dwindling in the Hallowed Halls", *Washington Post,* Monday: A3.
2.   Ibid. A3.
3.   Wolff, Robert Paul (1969). *The Ideal of the University.* Boston: Beacon Press: 131.

4. Dolan, Patrick (1976). *The Ranking Game*. Lincoln, Nebraska: University of Nebraska Printing and Duplicating Service.

5. Kolstoe, Oliver P. (1975). *College Professoring*. Carbondale: Southern Illinois University Press: 132.

6. Veblen, Thorstein (1957). *The Higher Learning In America*. New York: Hill and Wang, (Original published in 1918): 185-186.

7. Swazey, Judith P., Louise, Karen Seashore and Anderson, Melissa (1994). "The Ethical Training of Graduate Students Requires Serious and Continuing Attention," *The Chronicle of Higher Education*, March 9, 1994: B1 and B2.

8. Banks, McDonnell (1991). *Ethical Conduct and the Professional's Dilemma*. New York: Quorum Books: 3-4.

9. Gose, Ben (1994). "Lawsuit 'Feeding Frenzy", *The Chronicle of Higher Education*. August 17: A27-A28.

10. Barber, Benjamin R.(1992). *An Aristocracy of Everyone*. New York: Oxford University Press, 226-227.

11. Dewey, John (1916). *Democracy and Education*. New York: Macmillan.

12. Rudolph, Frederick (1962). *The American College and University*. New York: Vintage Books: 41, 125.

13. Herring, Mark Youngblood (1988). *Ethics and the Professor: An Annotated Bibliography, 1970-1985*. New York: Garland Publishing Company: 3-101. See chapter 1, *The Warnings of Conscience: Professional Ethics* which covers academic rank and tenure; professional ethics; academic values and education; governance; arbitration, and academic freedom.

14. Cahn, Steven M. (1994). *Ethics in Academia: Saints and Scamps*. Lanham, Maryland: Rowman and Littlefield Publishers.

15. Eble, Kenneth (1971). *The Recognition and Evaluation of Teaching*. Washington, D. C. American Association of University Professors: 16-18.

16. Cahn, *Ibid:* 42.

17. Stecklow, Steve (December 1, 1994). "Chief Prerequisite for College President's Job: Stamina", *Wall Street Journal,* Thursday: B1 and B10.

18. Brimelow, Peter (1993). "Are Universities Necessary?" *Forbes,* April 26:170.

Chapter 3

Academic Administrators

Now, as a matter of fact, university presidents, at least in our time, live about as far from the ivory tower as one can imagine. They confront reality day by day, hour by hour. They raise funds to balance budgets that may exceed half a billion dollars, negotiate with unions, cope with the individualisms of the professoriate and irrepressible ingenuity of students.

John Silber[1]

University presidents face an ever-increasing burden of balancing day-to-day pressures with the necessity for a vision of a university. The pressures have led to a shorter tenure for university presidents. Term in office varies from three to five years, with notable exceptions of some who remain in office more than a decade. One need only look at a current issue of the *Chronicle of Higher Education* to see the number of post-secondary institutions advertising for a chief executive officer. John Dewey noted that our schools are miniature societies. The challenges faced by the larger society are reflected in the problems brought into our colleges each day by faculty, staff and students. Various university constituencies each seek to push an agenda. Social protests over affirmative action, faculty fighting for their turf, for a larger portion of a smaller budget, AIDS, drug use and abuse, sexual harassment cases, gender equity and phasing out of mandatory retirement are but a few of the issues faced by college presidents.

Deans seek to gain more advantage for their schools, single interest groups seek special privileges, the public brings pressures to bear through their legislators to reform higher education and the board of trustees responds to pressures to put proposals into effect without consulting the institution's president. From Harvard to the University of Arkansas, Fayetteville, faculties protest attempts by the boards of trustees to reduce the heavier burden of health care costs. Faced by budgetary pressures, college boards of trustees often implement programs without adequately engaging the university community in dialogue. The end result is that faculty and staff feel the administration is imposing programs, rules, and regulations that affect them without involving them in decision making. Votes of no-confidence in the administration ring throughout the campuses. This puts the president in a difficult position since he or she may not have been adequately informed of the response of faculty and staff to a board's decision or did not realize the ramifications and multiplier effects of a decision.

In addition to these pressures, there are efforts to evaluate administrators. Faculty members who are evaluated yearly band together to require evaluation of college administrators. As Clark Kerr noted a few years ago in an address to the *American Association of Higher Education*, evaluation of college presidents may have an unintended multiplier effect. College presidents may be afraid to offend any of the various college populaces and thus become ineffective. The president may not take any action on urgent issues but rather delegate the problem to committees. Committees then make a lengthy study often concluding that the issue is important but needs further long-term study which effectively tables the issue.

It is clear that there is a need to protect administrators who face increasingly complex institutional problems. Many years ago when I was working with the *Agency for International Development,* an official would note that to be effective in a leadership position, to manage institutional change, and/or to create institutional visions, a person would have to be in a position for at least seven to ten years. With college presidents facing shorter tenure, many institutions are adrift, moving from one crisis to another without an adequate and firm grip on the leadership tiller. As our society seeks to find unity within diversity, higher education institutions' leaders find themselves confronted with heightened sensitivity of a larger number of single interest groups. Rutgers President Francis L. Lawrence's remarks about African Americans ability to do well on admissions tests, has led to demands for his resignation by student groups. As other educators before him had noted through the years, Lawrence saw the potential bias in tests that were not designed to be cultural free tests.

Notwithstanding his commitment to opening special study centers at Rutgers for Latino, Black, Puerto Rican, Hispanic and Caribbean studies and to increasing the number of minority students, student anger may well lead to his resignation. Lawrence's numerous apologies for remarks that were insensitive have been ineffective in fending off increasing criticism of his leadership at Rutgers[2]. Part of the student anger may be a general reaction to publications such as Charles Murray's book, *The Bell Curve,* which Geiger[3] suggests is using an age-old practice of attaching a negative label to entire groups of people and then using that label as an excuse for neglect or outright discrimination.

University presidents also are facing increased faculty surveillance regarding allocation of resources within the university, as administrators' salaries are questioned. Institutional researchers are more frequently called on to reveal the percentage of university budgets devoted to administrator salaries in the nation and region. Explanation and justification for resource allocation is a continuing effort by university presidents. Their responses often include needed fund raising efforts necessitating additional personnel as well as a growing number of governmental mandates, rules, and regulations. Among these are Americans with Disabilities Act in the 1991 Civil Rights Act, laboratory safety acts, asbestos abatement projects, and hazardous materials disposal acts. Although the percentage of resources used to address these issues varies according to the size of an institution, from 30% to 40% of the budget is a usual figure to deal with governmental safety and health regulations. The cost is higher for older institutions that have to engage in extensive remodeling of buildings to meet new accessibility rules for the disabled. These are social commitments made by the society at large and reflect an expanded social consciousness.

Universities and colleges are large communities, and many have larger budgets than small cities. Higher education administrators operate health centers, transportation facilities, housing and food services, book stores, fire and safety services, traffic and safety offices and police functions. With increasing incidents of violence in the larger society, student safety is a larger concern. All of these campus services need to operate within the parameters of a litigious society which requires a large legal contingency. In times of financial exigency, these services must be maintained.

Divisiveness in the society is reflected in universities in particularly strident tones. Various interest groups are seeking more of limited budgets for their special causes. In addition, some groups vehemently express their contempt for those of differing persuasions. "Political correctness" is a term used to express currently popular modes of belief and action. Occasionally, the friction between varying points of view leads to withdrawal of large donations as faculty seek to modify or change the intent of the donor in reference to allocation and distribution of funds. These added conflicts increase the pressure on university presidents and administrations. It is not unusual to see three or more administrations in three years, as occurred recently at Yale University. In a three-year period, Yale University had three administrations, three presidents and three provosts.

Governing Boards of Higher Education

Faced with increasing criticism of higher education, governing boards are exploring ways and means to increase employers' confidence in the states' higher education system. Recently administrators and governing boards in Oklahoma issued a draft, " Building on Success: The Next Step for Oklahoma Higher Education," which included a commitment to the development of warranties or guarantees that graduates could perform adequately in the workplace[4]. As in other states, Oklahoma plans to begin issuing institutional "report cards" disclosing employment rates and job performance of graduates of college and universities within the state. In an effort to seek needed additional funding from the legislature, educational officials want to demonstrate effective use of future funds. With rising demand and shrinking budgets, administrators face pressure to be responsive to changing market demands and to be accountable in the use of funds. Under the Oklahoma proposal for warranties or guarantees, the faculty and the corresponding business representative develop a list of competencies for each degree program. On graduation, the student's first employer is given a letter certifying that the student has mastered the list. If the employer is dissatisfied, the student will be given up to nine additional college hours at no additional cost. This system has been unsuccessfully tried before in other institutions. Other measures recommended by the Oklahoma higher education administrators include improving internal and external polling, surveys, public hearings, or any other forum that will increase communication between the public and the college and university[5].

Unless otherwise noted, the following information is from *Strategies for Improvement,* a report of the Arkansas State Board of Higher Education, adopted January 28, 1994, in Little Rock. In the fall of 1992, seven college and university administrators and three Arkansas Department of Higher Education representatives were appointed to an Institutional Productivity Committee by the president of the Arkansas Higher Education Council. The mission for the committee included finding ways for greater institutional accountability, methods of rewarding increased productivity, with attention given to statewide education goals, goal achievement and resulting funding policies. The philosophy of Total Quality Management was utilized to achieve continuous product improvement. The Committee noted that American higher education has been faced with two major themes in the past decade--institutional accountability and educational quality. To deal with these themes, the Delphi technique research method was used. This is a method by which individuals are divided into groups and work toward eventual consensus about the most important ways to deal with an issue or solve a problem. Seven goals for productivity enhancement resulted from the deliberations. The goals were:

(1) To increase retention of first-time, full-time award-seeking students at all levels of higher education. Special incentives were suggested to improve retention rates of first to second year students, with a focus on increased retention of minority students and those enrolled in developmental classes.
(2) To improve postsecondary graduation rates at the certificate, associate, and baccalaureate levels. Incentive funding was suggested, with emphasis on graduation rates of minority students and athletes across all disciplines.
(3) To improve the quality of academic programs at all levels: certificate, associate, bachelors, master's and doctoral. Efforts to improve program quality through external program reviews, licensure examination scores, program-specific exit examinations, and alumni/employer surveys with special incentives were recommended.
(4) To increase students' mastery level in general education areas as measured by rising junior examination scores, with special incentives for improvement.
(5) To improve the focus and allocation of resources based on institutional mission. It was the expectation that institutions would maintain quality and vitality while seeking ways to curb excessive or unnecessary administrative costs. Special incentives were to be provided for those institutions that increased program productivity and decreased the number of low productivity programs without sacrificing education quality. Included in this

goal was the increase of the average number of credit hours taught by full-time faculty.

(6) To achieve greater responsiveness of Arkansas higher education to the needs of business and industry.

(7) To provide special incentives for improving the racial diversity of faculty, administrative, and professional staff. As a means of achieving this goal, predominantly white institutions are to strive to increase the total number of African-American faculty and administrative staff and to continue to make improvement.

These recommendations were designed to achieve equity funding. A study of educational funding methods in the south reveal the complexities of funding for higher education. Unless otherwise noted, the following information is from J. Kent Caruthers and Joseph L. Marks' *Funding Methods For Public Higher Education in the SREB States,* Atlanta, Georgia: Southern Regional Board, 1994. Caruthers and Marks find that each state has its own history, traditions, and terminology. The most widely used methods for budgeting are "formulas" or quantitative statements that prescribe how to build a request for funding or allocating funds among institutions. Other methods are "incremental," "programmatic justification," and "categorical" funding. The authors surveyed the evolution of the objectives of funding methods over some four decades. Generally, each new decade's objective was an addition rather than a replacement purpose. Thus, although there is a move toward "equity" funding, the traditional FTE (full-time-equivalent) method continues to be used as part of the process of allocation of resources.

Evolution of the Objective of Funding Methods

Adequacy	→	Growth	→	Equity	→	Stability/Quality	→	Stability/Accountability/Reform
1950s		1960s		1970s		1980s		1990s

Funding methods in the twenty SREB (Southern Regional Education Board) states tend to rely on comparative data such as salary averages of peer institutions and quantitative elements such as student/faculty ratios to meet the objectives of adequacy, growth, and objectivity. The difficult challenge of achieving equity among institutions was generally reached by basing funding on differences in program structure and activity, adding mission, level, and program differentiation, making funding methods complex. There are two basic formats used in funding formulas: a dollar rate times a student credit hour or full-time-equivalent (FTE) student measure, and a student/faculty ratio times a salary rate or set of salary rates. In the SREB states, the first method is employed in ten states, the second method in five states, and five states employ a mixed method.

In the never-ending quest to assess teaching/learning effectiveness, several states have implemented various forms of an assessment examination generally given to undergraduate students enrolled in colleges and universities. An example of such assessment is Arkansas legislative Act 874 of 1993. The Act requires that the Arkansas Assessment of General Education be given to every student enrolled at four-year colleges and universities in programs requiring State Minimum Core of 35 hours. That includes all undergraduate students who are degree candidates. The test is to be given to students who have accumulated between 45 and 60 college-level credits. Students will be assessed a fee to take the test. There will be no pass/fail, but the test is to be used to measure and record student performance and will be used to compare institutions as to student test scores. Results of the test will be used to help determine how the Arkansas Department of Higher Education divides money among the state's colleges and universities. Work on the assessment process and procedures will continue to be refined as the project takes shape. Called the "rising junior test" developed and distributed by ACT, it will provide data for use as:

1. a basis for incentive funding to promote improvement in quality of curriculum and instruction.
2. one basis, among many, for assessment of student achievement, for review of program quality, and for improvement of teaching and learning.
3. a basis for reporting statewide results and overall improvement.

Once the data are available, incentive funding for assessment results will be based on: a) exceeding of national averages in at least three of the four test areas (reading, writing, mathematics, and scientific reasoning), b) improvement over the institutional total score baseline and c) a positive change in decile between pre-test and post-test in reading, writing, mathematics and scientific reasoning.

In recent years, quality concerns have been addressed in a variety of ways by implementing non-formula special initiatives such as endowed chairs, centers of excellence, and incentive funding. At the same time, ideally, governing boards have not overlooked the importance of and ideal of a seamless funding program from kindergarten to doctoral level institutions. State funding agencies have a moral and ethical obligation to assure young people equitable funding at all levels of the educational system. Pitting one educational sector against another for the larger share of a smaller fiscal pie is detrimental to all and beneficial to none.

The twenty Southern Regional Board States are a microcosm of the national picture of funding challenges for higher education. State economic woes, growing public investment in health care and criminal justice, and concerns about higher education accountability have generally caused state leaders to tighten education budgets and look for new ways to fund public colleges and universities. Questions about achieving a balance between teaching and research without shortchanging research continue to be debated.

Summary:

Higher education administrators face increased demands from a variety of agencies, pressure groups, and fund raising efforts. Bok[6] found that the role of leadership in the universities is difficult. The following information is from Bok's *Beyond the Ivory Tower* (1982), unless otherwise noted. Faculty members historically have had power to fix the curriculum, set academic requirements, search for new professors and shape admissions standards. Since Bok's book was written, there is a move toward hiring professional managers with a business background to be chief executive officers of universities, and historic turf areas may well be challenged. It is not uncommon to have boards of trustees engage professional management search teams to locate a president. Although faculty may feel offended by not having much input into a president's or chancellor's selection, board members often seek individuals with business management experience. Not infrequently a board member may note that he or she does not understand why a Ph.D. who wrote a dissertation on nuclear physics is a good candidate for a university presidency.

Students can exert pressures by attending schools they like and can change university policy by showing their disapproval. Alumni can block actions they do not want by withholding contributions. Government agencies at all levels can exert their collective will through regulatory power and allocation of the state's resources.

Changing composition of higher education boards of trustees can influence organizational climate and governance. As Mary Cage notes in *Calling It Quits*[7], Robert H. McCabe of Miami-Dade Community College received recognition and honors for his 15 years of leadership. She noted the college trustees supported his decisions, often referring to McCabe as a visionary. With a change in the composition of the board of trustees, his days were numbered, as the board sought to micromanage the organization. Cage notes that board of trustee members are seeking to become active managers rather than rubber stampers of the past. McCabe became a lighting rod for all kinds of criticism from faculty, staff and students. Faced with challenges of dealing with the public, the contentious board, financial restrictions, as well as the legislature, McCabe retired. His challenges suggest the difficult times that lie ahead for those who follow him. Future presidents will face the problems of meeting the many remedial needs for inter-city minority youth, the continuing search for funds in a more restrictive financial environment, and demands for raising standards as well as increasing financial incentives for faculty members. The challenge of retaining academic leaders may be difficult with the greater pressure to deal with management and political problems on campus.

Bok further noted that presidents and deans, although having shared authority, can exert influence, too. They can block programs or initiatives that might be detrimental to standards or quality or impinge on turf of other units of the university. Programs can be blocked if there is danger to other members of society. Care should always be taken to prevent arbitrary exercise of authority that would impinge on academic freedom. University presidents, according to Bok, ought to maintain neutrality when faced with groups pressing for various ideological goals. Any president or dean who fails to maintain neutrality in such a case violates his or her trust and probably will be confronted with opposition from faculty, alumni, and trustees.

Presidents and deans can exert a positive influence through encouraging innovative new ventures. Academic leaders should search for neglected opportunities and new initiatives for valuable work. When faced with political overtones of such initiatives, each new venture can be debated by the faculty. Participating scholars should be chosen for their academic merits. Such action will prevent the ventures from being used for predetermined ends.

John W. Gardner[8] In the *Anrloadorohip Taoomo* discusses challenges and opportunities of leadership positions. He found that mutual suspicion is just about as common as mutual respect and that most of the significant issues in our society are settled by a balancing of forces. Most leaders, Gardner notes, are hedged by constraints such as tradition, rights and privileges of followers, and requirements of large scale organizations. Gardner noted that many leaders work to determine how they can reach a decision without really deciding. They may send an issue through various committees within an organization to table or settle it. Gardner found that regardless of what individuals would like, they cannot do without leaders.

> It is the nature of social organization that we must have them at all levels....in education and every other field. Since we must have them, it helps considerably if they are gifted in the performance of their appointed task. The sad truth is that a great many of our organizations are badly managed or badly led. And because of that, people within those organizations are frustrated when they need not be frustrated. They are not helped when they could be helped. They are not given the opportunities to fulfill themselves that are clearly possible (p.11-12).

Gardner concludes by calling for leadership that serves to define and articulate the most cherished social and individual human goals that our society values so highly---in other words moral leadership. This moral leadership can serve to express the values that hold society together, to articulate goals that lift people out of their petty preoccupations, carry them above the conflicts that tend to tear society apart, and unite them in the pursuit of objectives worthy of their best efforts (p. 12).

Case Studies:

Case #1
A Time Factor

An untenured professor, Henry Burke, had a good teaching record. He had taught at a large midwestern college with 10,000 students for three years. The academic dean sent a memo informing him that a student had reported Burke for having held his class five minutes longer than the assigned period and that the complaint would be entered in his personnel file and sent to his department head. The student reported it was difficult to get to her next class on time. Burke, a sensitive dedicated scholar, was chagrined. Student complaints, no matter how minor, were utilized by the administration in determination of yearly resource allocation among faculty. Frequently students engaged in discussions after the class period. The class schedule was arranged to allow some limited deviation from the allotted time. He was unsure how to respond other than to indicate unforeseen student questions and discussion had prolonged the class period. This had not happened before in the three years Burke had been at the college.

Discussion:

What administrative theory was behind the Dean's action? What response should Burke make? Discuss pros and cons of the faculty oversight.

Case #2
A Route to Power

At a major midwestern college of some 24,000 students, a newly appointed dean, James Jones, asked all department heads to submit their resignation in writing by the end of the week. Department heads were dismayed. The institution had a record of employment stability, and several department heads had served in their positions for more than twenty years. Each had a conference with the dean, and most were retained in their position.

Discussion:

What leadership theory was the Dean espousing? Does this suggest a method of acquiring and holding power? Would you have handled the first day on the job differently? What effect do you think the Dean's action had on morale at the College?

Case #3
Micromanagement

Hank Smith, a middle level central administrator, served as head of his research division. He had good relationships with those who served under him and took pride in his collegial relationships with his superiors. A new chancellor hired several assistants, one of whom, Mary Jones, was appointed to supervise Smith's division among others. Carrying a beeper and setting up a communication system to constantly monitor Smith's daily activities, Jones micromanaged the division. She also maintained constant communication with the chancellor through her communication system. Smith found himself having to backtrack on commitments, assignments, and research he had endorsed. It led to anxiety, frustration, and a feeling his work was no longer accepted as a professional. He approached Mary several times to ameliorate the situation. She was extremely authoritarian, overly concerned with her administrative powers and insisted on thorough oversight of Smith's own decisions at all times. Highly competent, with an excellent record of achievement and commitment to the university over a period of some 30 years, he resigned to serve another institution in the same capacity. He had thought of approaching the Chancellor about his job problems. The Chancellor was an excellent public relations administrator and fund raiser. However, the Chancellor found it hard to make decisions and left that process to his administrative assistants.

Discussion:

How would you have handled the situation? Would you have sought more persistently to communicate morale concerns to Mary? Should the university have an ombudsman system to deal with conflicts? A conflict management system?

Case #4
Who is in Charge Here?

A mid-level administrator at a major southwestern university with more than 40,000 students has been involved in the production of a national survey of institutions for 19 years. In all, the survey had been in production for nearly 30 years. The survey received an exceptionally high participation rate from peer institutions. Each participating institution received a complimentary copy of the study and additional copies were sold to participants or other interested parties. As the high participation rate indicated, the survey publication was widely utilized and recognized by institutions as a valuable information resource. The sales of copies of the report more than paid for the cost of the study. The survey has been noted by librarians of the University as being one of the few entries from the state regularly reported in ERIC (Education Resources Information Center). The producing administrator received special awards in recognition of the study. Refinement of techniques and data input reduced time and resource requirements virtually every year for the last six years.

The unit conducting the study found itself reporting to new and different administrators about every other year for the last six years. Each new administrator threatened to require the office to discontinue its national survey to concentrate on their own plans and innovations. Campus administrators did not recognize the value placed on the survey by administrators across the country. They each had their own individual agenda. The mid-level administrator was faced with conflicting messages from various administrators and found it difficult to find who was in charge.

Discussion:

How should mid-management respond to excessive micromanagement? Why would administrators seek to abolish a self maintained and worthy contribution to scholarship? What administrative theory is represented by the case? Does this case suggest that anything can be done in a large university with little effect on the overall operation of the organization? Does this case suggest why so many changes occur within the ranks of mid-management at major universities?

Case #5
What Do We Do Next?

A chief executive officer of a major northern state university was demonstrating symptoms of forgetfulness. He would be seen frequently wandering the halls. Some faculty members consulted with the janitors and found that the university president was having some difficulty finding his office. He would frequently ask the university janitors for help in locating his office. No one wished to raise an issue about the problem, but as it became more noticeable, both faculty, middle level administration and staff wondered how effective the chief executive officer was in making decisions that affected the institution. He had led the institution for over 35 years in good times and bad. Although much respected for his leadership, he had always exercised a very firm grip on the institution and created a climate not conducive to analyzing or questioning executive actions.

Discussion:

What should faculty, administrators, and staff members all of whom were aware of the situation do? Should they take it to the board, or should they wait and see how things worked out? Those who worked most closely with the president noticed some changes in his behavior but were hesitant to rock the boat. What would you do if you were a close associate of the president?

Case Study #6
How Best to Make A Decision

A new associate director was hired to run a program that would support research and curriculum development. The position was a newly created position at a mid-sized, state-supported institution (averaging 9,000 students over the past five years). The program was created about five years previously and had grown from a staff of a part-time director, part-time accountant, and part-time graduate assistant to the part-time director, one associate director, one secretary, one part-time accountant, and two part-time graduate assistants. The funds had grown from less than $500,000 to over $2.6 million in grants.

The new associate director decided that the administration of the office should be transferred from a manual system to a computerized system. The old recording and reporting systems, which were being done manually, had been developed by the director. Since access to the computer programmers on campus was not a viable option, a commercially developed computerized software package which was designed for the administration of a grant's office was purchased. However, the new software package would not provide all of the same information as the old system, nor would the software package provide information in the same format as did the old manual system.

Discussion:

Assuming that the new computerized system did not leave out pertinent information in the opinion of the associate director, should the associate director recommend the transfer of the systems? If so, what possible pitfalls exist? What steps should be taken to eliminate these pitfalls or at least minimize any negative effects?

Case Study #7
An Experience Factor?

A supervisor at the Coordinating Board of Higher Education had been employed for several years, always getting an excellent evaluation by managers. However, a new manager was employed who had no administrative or managerial experience. That lack of experience led the new manager to practice a leadership style that was very domineering and controlling. The new manager also practiced favoritism with employees who built up the manager's ego. The supervisor decided not to cater to the manager's ego, but to continue working as before and to maintain a professional manner with the manager. However, the manager responded with refusing travel requests, cutting the supervisor's budget, and eventually giving the supervisor a very low evaluation. Since the evaluation would become a permanent part of the supervisor's personnel record, the supervisor first approached the manager and then the manager's supervisor. The manager refused to change the evaluation. The manager's supervisor advised ignoring the evaluation because it is "only one bad evaluation out of several years of excellent evaluations".

Discussion:

How should the supervisor have handled the situation? Based on events so far, what should the supervisor do now? What are the pros and cons of any action? If the supervisor's complaints are valid, then what action should the manager's supervisor take?

Case Study #8
Handling a Complaint

Mary Smith found that her professor, Elaine Wilson, had graded her examination in error. She immediately took it to professor Wilson to point out the error which led to a lower grade on the test than she had legitimately earned. Elaine Wilson after examining the test score agreed with the student that an error had been made. The faculty member, however, refused to change the grade since she would have had to change other grades in class. After repeated efforts to get the professor to correct the error proved to no avail, the student entered her complaint with the department chair. The chair supported Elaine Wilson. The student then went to the Dean with her complaint.

Discussion:

How should the dean respond to the legitimate student complaint? Dr. Wilson was a new faculty member. The dean wanted to give her maximum support yet he had to resolve the student complaint. The student also was ready to take her complaint to the Vice-Chancellor for Academic Affairs. What would you do in the circumstances?

References

1. Silber, John (1974). *Straight Shooting,* New York: Harper & Row: xii.
2. Wilson, Robin (1995). "Flashpoint at Rutgers U", *Chronicle of Higher Education,* February 24: A21.
3. Geiger, Keith (1994). "The Bell Curve Rings False", *The Christian Science Monitor,* Monday, November 14: 18.
4. Krehbiel, Randy (December 23, 1994). "Regents Eye Warranty", *Tulsa World*, Saturday : 1, 3.
5. *Ibid:* 3.
6. Bok, Derek (1982). *Beyond the Ivory Tower,* Cambridge, Massachusetts: Harvard University Press.
7. Cage, Mary Crystal (August 11, 1995). "Calling It Quits", *The Chronicle of Higher Education:* A 15-A16.

8. Gardner, John, (1965). *The Antileadership Vaccine*, New York: Carnegie Corporation of New York.

Chapter 4

The Professoriate

Simpson and Thomas[1] stress the importance of collegiality, community, and diversity in our colleges and universities. They note that all of us want to feel good about ourselves and our organizations. Respect, trust, and being treated as an equal should be routine in organizations. However, in a competitive society there is often conflict at all levels, at all times, and in all places. Hacker[2] addresses part of this conflict by identifying some of the challenges of providing education in a period of restricted finances. He finds the biggest item in college budgets, tenured faculty salaries, are virtually untouchable while part-time lecturers receive pink slips. Hacker's complaint is that "full-professor bloat" leaves colleges and universities with little money left to hire or retain younger people without tenure. Bennett[3] addresses the issue of tenure noting that Bennington College dismissed 27 of its 80 professors and announced tenure would not be given to new employees. Then the college hired new teachers on one-year contracts. Bennett notes that some college administrators and state governments find the practice of tenure reduces flexibility and protects the unproductive. He cites Boston University President, John Silber, who finds that in universities if you want to terminate a professor you have to prove "utter incompetence." Some professors have questioned the value of tenure and younger faculty complain that tenure clogs career paths with older professors making their best salaries while their productivity may be declining. Bennett finds that even with all the complaints about tenure as an "outmoded concept", over

97% of all four-year colleges offer tenure; university administrators seek tenure in an academic department prior to being hired, and competition for top flight professors is so keen at large universities that tenure cannot be abolished. Bennett interviewed John Silber on the question of tenure and found that all top flight candidates insist on tenure and "you can't be competitive if you don't offer tenure."

Senior faculty members complain about salary compression. While their salaries remain flat or increase below the cost of inflation index, younger faculty are hired at assistant professor rank with higher salaries. In addition, senior faculty hired under a different philosophy that stressed off-campus teaching, heavy work loads, organizational loyalty and dedication to service, now face new demands for research, grant acquisition, and publication. Thus, for years of dedicated service, senior faculty are unrewarded. They are often viewed by younger faculty as nonproductive and unworthy of continued employment.

Senior faculty are viewed as unmovable furniture that sometimes gets in the way, while junior faculty are given reduced workloads, financial incentives for research, computers, and other needed equipment. When a transition occurs from a philosophy of service to a philosophy of competitive research and grant acquisition, it is a challenging time for faculty whose lives have been dedicated to an institution. Within ten years or so, the situation will resolve itself as senior faculty phase out and the new agenda takes center stage. A student of higher educational history, however, might predict a switch back to service in the years ahead. The new President of the University of Oklahoma at Norman, David Boren, is seeking to work with restricted finances by rehiring retired faculty to teach undergraduate courses.

The junior faculty faces morale problems as well. Having received reduced workloads for high research productivity, they feel intense pressure to produce. Many younger faculty members are opting out of major research universities. They would rather function in non-competitive environments for their own and their families' health. Thus, four year colleges and non-research schools are able to recruit top flight faculty. Other faculty members refuse to play the competitive game, stay until they come up for tenure which varies by institution, and then move to other institutions. This is particularly true for minorities and women. Tack and Patitu[4] note that in the competitive market for women and minorities, there is a need for creative deployment of resources together with innovative ways of attracting and retaining talented women and minority faculty. Tack and Patitu call for an environment attractive and conducive to job satisfaction and success for women and minorities. They stress the importance of sabbaticals, above-market salaries, released time for research, child care provisions, reduced teaching and committee loads, plus flexible promotion and tenure schedules to assure tenure and full professorial rank.

Research Studies

Tang and Chamberlain[5] conducted a survey of attitudes toward teaching and research with 230 administrators and 384 faculty members at six regional Tennessee state universities. Administrators agree more strongly than faculty members that research is essential, teaching is essential, teaching is rewarded, teaching effectiveness is related to survival, teaching and research are mutually supportive, and rewards influence performance. Administrators also agree more strongly that less research would be done if tenure were not based on research productivity, and that the university needs to hire faculty members with strength in both research and teaching. Faculty, on the other hand, agreed more strongly than administrators that research is rewarded, that research productivity is related to survival, that research interferes with teaching, that teaching offers satisfaction, and that universities need to hire faculty members with strength in either teaching or research.

Bieber, Lawrence, and Blackburn[6] interviewed the University of Michigan's College of Literature, Sciences and the Arts faculty to determine changing themes in faculty life. New trends in faculty promotion emerged. Formerly, assistant professors had to achieve a strong publication record to earn promotion and then could coast toward eventual retirement as full professors. Currently, faculty members must maintain a strong record in order to survive additional rounds of tenure-like review for promotion. The use of multiple criteria for promotion has been abandoned and only research productivity matters. A second theme that emerged was the collegial environment where faculty members perceive new norms based on ambition, competitiveness, and a career professional orientation. As a result of these changes, faculty members perceive that the university has lost some of its essential community characteristics. Fairweather[7] in a analysis of data from the 1987-88 National Survey of Post Secondary Faculty revealed that in four-year colleges and universities, average salaries were highest for faculty members who taught less that 35% of the time and lowest for faculty members who taught at least 72% of the time. Those who spent less than six hours a week teaching earned an average of $40,927, while those who spent 12 hours or more a week teaching class earned an average of $36, 793. Except at liberal arts colleges, faculty income drops as the number of student contact hours per semester increases. Faculty who taught only graduates, who spent most of their time on research and scholarship, and those who have the most refereed publications throughout their career earned more on average than their counterparts. Research and scholarship models were the dominant reward structure for all types of institutions. Full professors received more pay for publishing and spending more time on research and less time on teaching. Associate professors earned more based on research, administrative duties and teaching. In the liberal arts colleges, teaching was a negative factor in compensation for professors at all ranks.

Daly[8] refers to a report derived from the work of the *Institute For Scientific Information* that notes the limited amount of published research that is ever used and cited, even by other academic researchers. He notes that one research report estimated that of all the articles published in even the most prestigious natural and social science journals, less than half were ever read by anyone, that less than one-fifth were cited more than once, and that many of the meager number of citations that were garnered were the result of self citations by authors in subsequent publications of their own. Daly finds that there is the possibility that much of the published research the professoriate has felt itself compelled to generate has never been read or cited by anyone. He reports that one-half of the respondents in the Carnegie study felt that their publications were merely counted, never read, even by those who insist on those same publications as a prerequisite for tenure or promotion.

There are indications that the public and legislatures are calling for more teaching. More state legislatures are analyzing time spent in teaching and seeking more productivity and accountability measures. Walters[9] reports some university professors work 60-65 hours a week, but only 12 of those hours are spent teaching students in class. The Ohio legislature has passed a law requiring a 10 percent increase in teaching at the state's 13 public universities. Parents and legislatures are expressing concern about graduate assistants teaching classes, and at least 12 state legislatures have mandated studies of faculty workload at public universities in the past several years. A problem Walters identified was that with the expansion of higher education all kinds of institutions have worked to become research oriented. The difficulty of legislating a specific amount of time to be given to teaching fails to take into account the unique enterprise of college instruction. Research and teaching may well be intertwined. Good teachers need to keep up-to-date in their field. Attending professional association meetings, giving papers in their field of interest and expertise, and publishing in peer reviewed journals serve to enrich the knowledge base for faculty. Networking with other faculty in the field may stimulate individuals to enrich the teaching enterprise. In addition, in research universities, faculty assist, encourage, and provide opportunities for graduate students to attend professional meetings, engage in networking with potential employers as well as present and publish their research. These activities greatly accelerate the move toward excellence and quality in the teaching-learning enterprise.

Faculty ranking systems are often the result of legislative mandated merit systems. As Lublin[10] points out, however, accountability and productivity models based on rankings are being rethought in the business community. He finds that bosses hate to give them, and workers hate to get them. Lublin relates that one senior executive at a big automaker so dreaded face to face evaluations he recently delivered a manager's review while both sat in adjoining stalls in the men's room. The boss told the startled employee that he was going to receive a bonus of 20% and that he was happy with his work. Lublin finds that AT&T has stopped assigning performance rankings to about 37,000 U.S. managers. AT&T's five rating categories, "unsatisfactory" to "exceeds objectives," sometimes fostered internal rivalry and discouraged teamwork. Other companies wrestling with the evaluation issue are dropping routine evaluations except for problem cases. It is clear that evaluations are essential in an age of litigation especially in cases of dismissal, promotion, or salary distribution, and efforts will continue to be made to make them more effective. Unfortunately, the collegial atmosphere of the university will be restricted, as more productivity, merit and accountability measures are mandated by state legislatures. While some might see the issue as a reflection of a "mean-spirited" society, others would dream of implementing a "love, worth, and recognition" society as suggested by William Glasser in *Deschooling Society.*

Faculty and administration in higher education have an obligation to disseminate information to the public, legislatures and public opinion catalysts on what function universities serve in a free society. It is as Veblen noted, not appropriate to apply the business/industrial model to a university. Emerging mandated productivity formulas are vague and difficult to implement without adding layer after layer of bureaucracy to higher education. Administrators and faculty ideally ought to be working as a team to inform the public of the central mission of a college and university in an open society.

Case Studies

Case #1
A Not So Subtle Hint

A professor, John Smith, at a major research university approached the Dean with recommendations for strengthening his department by allocating resources for new positions. The Dean was approached just before a major accrediting agency visit, and he was noticeably agitated. The following day, the faculty member had a job advertisement on his desk, with a note from the Dean indicating he thought this would be a good position for John. Over the next two weeks two additional job advertisements were placed on Professor Smith's desk by the Dean.

Discussion:

How should the faculty member have approached the issue? What would you have done in response to the Dean's action? Discuss the effect of such action on faculty morale. What administrative model was at work here? Authoritarian? Democratic? Charismatic? Other?

Case #2
What Are the Limits to Academic Freedom

A senior tenured professor, after many years in his position at a major Western University, started writing letters to the editors of local papers stating that many administrators were incompetent and totally unqualified because of lack of scholarship credentials. He continued harping on the lack of qualifications of administrators identifying them in all the local newspapers by name.

Discussion:

How far does academic freedom (freedom to teach and learn without interference) go? Did the professor exceed the bounds of academic freedom? How should other faculty members as professionals respond to this action? Please note that after a number of articles appeared in the state's newspapers and on local TV channels, the state legislature began examining ways to eliminate tenure.

Case #3
Divergence Between Theory and Practice

An informal policy within a college supported hiring from without rather than from within. This policy was designed to eliminate inbreeding in the institution. However, various departments within the college, continually hired recent graduates of their own areas. Others held to the policy.

Discussion:

Why would the policy in regard to hiring be ignored by some departments and upheld by others? Does inbreeding matter in a college or university? Are there circumstances that would suggest it is important to hire from within the ranks of the university? Identify these instances. Does hiring from the ranks of its own graduates improve the public image and relations of the university? In this instance is the problem a lack of a central communication system, or are policies tentative and to be interpreted according to individual circumstances?

Case #4
The Job Search

Professor Maggie Jones had taught for over 8 years as a graduate assistant, part time-instructor, two years as a temporary instructor, and four years as an assistant professor. She loved teaching, received outstanding student evaluations, spent evenings and week-ends preparing for class lectures and keeping up to date in her field of sociology. Jones, Ph.D. in hand, left her position and moved to a community with a major research university. She applied for a position in the sociology department but was told she needed to have an extensive research and grant acquisition record. Jones raised the question, "How can young Ph.D. graduates develop a publication record when most of their time is spent in meeting class and dissertation research requirements?" She wondered how potential faculty members could find time and funding to publish and attend and present papers at professional association meetings. Heartbroken and needing a job, she went back to graduate school to prepare for a position in a public high school.

Discussion:

What obligations, if any, do academic departments have to prepare their Ph.D. and Ed.D. graduates for the job market? How would you respond to the dilemma Jones faced? Is the issue overproduction of graduate students or overexpectation in the employment market? Is there a discrepancy between theory and practice in reference to balance between research and teaching? What do you see as the fundamental mission of the university--research, teaching, service or a combination? If a combination, what percentage of time should be devoted to each?

Case #5
Retaliation for Overseas Service

Timothy Land had been a faculty member for more than 20 years in a major research northeastern university with some 35,000 students. He had an opportunity to teach and engage in research in his field of specialization in Paris. He sought and received a leave of absence to work in Paris. In his view, it would reflect high credit on his department, college, and university. At the end of one year, he still had research to complete, and asked for another leave of absence. His department chair turned down the request, and he went to the Vice Chancellor for Academic Affairs to get another year's leave of absence. The leave was granted. On return to the department, the chairperson was definitely hostile and assigned Land 15 hours of teaching rather than the traditional 9 hours within the department. In addition, two of the courses were to be taught some 6 to 9 hours driving distance from the main campus. Land fulfilled all demands placed on him, but nothing changed the chairperson's hostile attitude and actions. Eventually Land was eased out of the department through a reduction in force. The university, however, had a policy of retraining, recycling or reallocating faculty who had their positions cut. Land served in another college with distinction until his retirement.

Discussion:

How would you have responded to the excessive demands placed on a returning faculty member who had an opportunity for a prestigious assignment? Should Land have appealed to the next administrative level to resolve the conflict? Should Land have filed grievance claims in reference to his unprofessional treatment? What should universities do to eliminate conflicts and resolve them in a professional manner? How is it possible for such adversarial issues to arise within an environment dedicated to the needs, interests, and concerns of people?

Case #6
Salary Compression

Bob Jeffers, an assistant professor, was hired in a college of a major western university of some 45,000 students. His salary was $34,000. In 1994, three years after Bob was hired, new assistant professors received $40,000. Bob spent more time than any other faculty member in the college counseling, advising, and assisting doctoral students and peers in research. He wondered if there would ever be a salary adjustment to deal with the issue of salary compression. Central administration based their hiring salaries on market conditions and availability of faculty within specialized academic areas. As Bob viewed the future, he felt the only way he could correct his salary imbalance was to move to another institution. He loved the community, his work, and his college but was unable to continue to support his family on a diminishing wage base that did not keep up with inflation.

Discussion:

Does the university have an obligation to keep exemplary scholars who contribute to the research base of the institution? Many professors in the nation are facing issues of salary compression. What do you think should be done, and how should university boards of trustees respond to the issue?

Case #7
Grading Practices

Jim Johns, a department head at a satellite campus, started getting a lot of feedback and discussion from students that the professors' grading practices were very different, although they were teaching the same course. Some of the students had complained to the department head about the harshness of Dr. Johnson's grading and the relative ease of completing the course in Dr. Kendrick's class with an "A." Some of the girls in Dr. Kendrick's class believed the boys got "better" grades.

Discussion:

What options does the department head have in this circumstance? Discuss professionalism and the right of faculty members to teach without interference on the basis of their expertise. How would professional administrators respond to these complaints? Should they be supportive of the professional expertise of their faculty? Do the professors have an obligation to teach the same material and expect similar results? Do they have academic freedom? How/or should you go about ensuring equal evaluations and results from students? Is it your "job" to do it"? Explain your options and what you chose to do.

Case 8
Group Think in Action

A senior faculty member had been teaching for more than thirty years. He had always required multiple choice, essay tests and required research papers for his classes. A faculty team received a grant to explore innovative teaching methods including qualitative evaluation through portfolios. The team by consensus decided to eliminate all traditional grading measures and installed a series of portfolio reports during the semester. The senior faculty member did his best to follow the new innovative evaluation procedure becoming more frustrated. The portfolio method included continued student evaluations of the faculty member. The senior faculty member wondered if professionalism in higher education meant other than group think, team approaches, or cooperative instruction.

Discussion:

Does the portfolio method have content validity? Are innovative teaching methods worth the cost in time and resources? Will innovative teaching methods that exclude traditional forms of testing students lead to increased grade inflation. Are higher education populations intrigued by new fads, experimental methods that may be detrimental to the **Ideal of the University** as a societal institution dedicated to preserving the best ideals of humankind, and exploring new frontiers for truth? Are administrators, faculty and students too enamored with cheap, quick, technological fixes to complex problems?

Case 9
The Quest for Tenure

Arnold P. is a fourth year assistant professor at a moderately sized university. During his four years, he has been recognized for his teaching and service. Additionally, Arnold has published an adequate number of publications and done a sufficient number of presentations that his department and college both recommended him for tenure and promotion. When his folio reached the vice-chancellor's level, Arnold was recommended for promotion but told that in spite of past practice, he couldn't be considered for tenure for at least two more years. Arnold knows that he must receive tenure in two years or leave the university. He knows that academic custom and usage at the institution granted tenure with his publication and presentation record. He knows what the appeal process is at his university.

Discussion:

Should he appeal or simply continue working and apply in two more years for tenure? The change in university policy has created a morale problem, and faculty members are not sure how to proceed. What would you do when confronted with the problem?

Case 10
Student Plagiarism

Adrian R. is an associate professor at a major university. She has taught at several other universities and has acquired tenure at her current school. Adrian serves as the director of several master's theses and is active on campus faculty committees. During the past year, she worked with a student who plagiarized a section of his thesis. Adrian recognized this and provided the student with the opportunity to change the section and to resubmit his work. The student has challenged Adrian saying that she simply does not like to work with male students and charging that she has a vendetta against him stemming from some verbal challenges to her teaching of theory in which he engaged while in one of her classes.

Discussion:

Should Adrian bring charges against the student? Should she call the committee and ask other professors to become involved? Should she resign as director of the thesis committee in favor of another faculty member? Is there another more preferable alternative?

Case #11
The Search for A Job

Casey S. is an instructor at a small college. He has been teaching at the college for nine years. During that time, he has always been viewed as an excellent teacher. Additionally, he has done a fair amount of writing and tries to serve on campus committees, although those positions are generally reserved for tenure track faculty. Casey has applied for a position which is tenure track and has made the initial cut.

Discussion:

Casey is concerned that his interview is simply a courtesy since he has been on campus for some time. (Casey finished his doctorate the past summer.) What type of information and references should he offer in order to enhance the possibility of acquiring the job? If he is not selected for the position, what should he do?

References

1. Simpson, Douglas and Thomas, Cornell (1993). "Community, Collegiality, & Diversity: Professors, Priorities, and Perversity", in James Van Patten, Editor, *Understanding the Many Faces of the Culture of Higher Education* Lewiston, New York: The Edwin Mellen Press, 17-32.

2. Hacker, Andrew (1992). "Too Many Full Professors: A Top-Heavy Pyramid", *The Chronicle of Higher Education,* March 4: B1, B2.

3. Bennett, Amanda (1994). " Tenure: Many Will Decry It, Few Deny It", *Wall Street Journal,* Monday, October 16, B7, B 10.

4. Tack, Martha W. and Patitu, Carol L. (1992). *Women and Minorities in Peril,* Washington, D.C.: Clearing House On Higher Education.

5. Tang, T. L. & Chamberlain, M. (1993). "Perceptual Differences Between Administrators and Faculty Members on Teaching and Research", paper given at *Southeastern Psychological Association,* Atlanta, March.

6. Bieber, J. P. , Lawrence, J.H. and Blackburn, R.T. (1992). " Through the Years: Faculty and Their Changing Institution", *Change,* 24 (July/August) 28-35.

7. Fairweather, James S. (1993). "Teaching, Research, and Faculty Rewards: A Summary of the Research Findings of the Faculty Profile Project," *National Center on Postsecondary Teaching, Learning and Assessment, Research Report.*

8. Daly, William T. (1994). "Teaching and Scholarship", *Journal of Higher Education,* Vol. 65., No 1 (January/February):47. (See also D. Hamilton (1990). "Publishing by-----and for---- the Numbers." *Science* 250, 7 December 1990, 1331-2 and E. Boyer (1990) *Scholarship Reconsidered.* Princeton: N.J.: Carnegie Endowment for the Advancement of Teaching).

9. Walters, Laurel Shaper (1995). "Publish or Perish Becomes Teach or Perish", *The Christian Science Monitor,* Monday, February 27:13.

10. Lublin, Joann S. (1994). "It's Shape Up Time for Performance Reviews", *Wall Street Journal,* Monday, October 3:B1.

Chapter 5

Affirmative Action: Retrospect and Prospect

The issue of the natural inequality of individuals was struggled with over 2,000 years ago when Aristotle[1] found that individuals were by nature unequal with different talents, skills, and intellectual abilities. The course in life that an individual takes is decided by one's own inclinations, talents, social circumstances, and by what one's associates appreciate and encourage. Thus, natural assets and social opportunities influence decisions an individual eventually takes. Aristotle found that how much one learns and how far one educates his or her native abilities depends on both intellectual capacity and the motivation for realization of achievement.

The United States has a history of expanded social consciousness as the government seeks, through its social institutions, to expand access to opportunities for more of its people. Minorities, women, the aged, youth and those challenged with exceptionality have been provided with ways and means for self-respect and self-esteem. One of the factors expanding the nation's social consciousness has been and continues to be governmental legislation. From the *Old Deluder Satan Act* of 1647, providing for schools whenever there were 50 families (elementary) and 100 families (secondary), to the Civil Rights Acts of 1957, 1963, 1964, 1968, and 1991, legislation has paved the way for social, political, and economic advance. Affirmative action programs in education generally fall under Title VII of the *Civil Rights Act of 1964* and Title IX of the *Education Amendments of 1972*. Under Executive Order 11246, issued in 1965, federal government contractors with 50 employees and $50,000 in contracts, as well as banks and certain other employers, are required to prepare written affirmative action programs. These programs are audited by the *Office of Federal Contract Compliance Programs* of the U.S. Department of Labor.

In the fall of 1989, the Department of Labor started investigating the composition and practices of corporate management to identify artificial barriers based on attitudinal or organizational bias that prevent qualified individuals from advancing to management level positions within their organizations[2]. Interspersed between these years were the *Equal Pay Act* of 1963, *Voting Rights Act* of 1965, *Age Discrimination Act* of 1967 and 1975, *Education Amendments* of 1972, *Rehabilitation Act* of 1973, *Equal Opportunities Act* of 1974, and *American Indian Religious Freedom Act* of 1978. These acts were based on principles of distributive and procedural justice which Aristotle had addressed through his writings.

A Theory of Justice

John Rawls in his *Theory of Justice*[3] identified two principles and two priority rules of justice. First, each person is to have an equal right to the most extensive total system of equal basic liberties compatible with a similar system of liberty for all. Second, social and economic inequalities are to be arranged so that they are both: (a) to the greatest benefit of the least advantaged, and (b) attached to offices and positions open to all under conditions of fair equality of opportunity. Priorities identified by Rawls were, first, liberty can be restricted only for the sake of liberty. Two cases that he noted under this priority rule were (a) a less extensive liberty must strengthen the total system of liberty shared by all, and (b) a less than equal liberty must be acceptable to those with the lesser liberty. The second priority rule noted that an inequality of opportunity must enhance the opportunities of those with the lesser opportunity and an excessive rate of saving must, on balance, mitigate the burden of those with fewer opportunities. The sum of transfers and benefits from essential public good should be arranged so as to enhance the expectations of the least favored consistent with the required savings and maintenance of equal liberties. When the basic structure takes this form, the distribution that results will be just (or not unjust). Each receives that total income (earnings plus transfers) to which he or she is entitled under the public system of rules, upon which his legitimate expectations are founded.

Rawls' general principle of justice was that all social primary goods-- liberty and opportunity, income and wealth, and the basis of self-respect-- are to be distributed equally unless an unequal distribution of any or all of these goods is to the advantage of the least favored.

Thus, there is distributive justice as well as procedural justice to assure that social institutions administer impartially and fairly in a just system. Rawls is underlining the importance of justice as fairness. In a larger sense, western liberalism expresses the effort of governments to encourage institutions to make provisions for those who have been excluded from opportunities to enjoy the full benefits of upward social mobility.

A Reexamination of Affirmative Action

Joseph Coates[4], a futurist, finds in his analysis of distribution of goods that more than two-thirds of African-Americans now have their foot on the ladder of upward mobility and, therefore, the issue has become not access but performance. There is an increasing concern about political correctness in society and a backlash against affirmative action because of perceptions that governmental, legislative, and legal protections may have had unintended effects in the market place. There are an increasing number of lawsuits dealing with reverse discrimination. At the same time, it is clear that business, industry, and educational institutions are, of necessity, expanding their efforts to deal with an increasing cultural and ethnic diversity in the United States. Frank and DeLisser[5] identify research showing that income and employment statistics reveal that most blacks have made only modest gains over the past 30 years. They refer to a study on the economics of affirmative action by the *Joint Center for Political and Economic Studies,* a Washington think tank, which concludes that while affirmative action programs are important in opening new opportunities for some blacks, the effects on employment and wages have been small. It is clearly difficult to engage in research on the subject since there is no way to determine what percentage of workers were hired specifically because affirmative action obligations

The 1994 Congressional election may lead to reexamination of the affirmative action efforts that have been in place for over 40 years. Julnes[6] reports that a number of school attorneys are finding that some of the Office of Civil Rights rules exceed statutory authority and erroneously require *affirmative action by school districts for certain students with disabilities.* Although this is a technical legal issue, the Office of Civil Rights as well as the Department of Education may well come under increasing scrutiny as the new Republican majority in Congress begins to implement its contract with America. There will be testimony by small business persons underlining the challenge of meeting increasing rules and regulations from governmental agencies and offices. In most cases, individuals issuing these regulations are non-elected officials interpreting and implementing various legislative acts.

Differing Perceptions

It is clear that individuals perceive the concept of affirmative action differently. Opp[7], in a study comparing perceptions of minority and white academic affairs vice presidents about barriers and approaches to minority faculty recruitment and retention, found that white administrators emphasize structural institutional barriers while minority administrators emphasize attitudinal barriers. Opp suggested promoting faculty equity through hiring minorities for top level community college administrative positions.

Rodriguez[8] finds that affirmative action policy in hiring black and Hispanic college faculty is still controversial among middle class black faculty who have benefited from it. This often is due to misconceptions about affirmative action and, to some, it connotes preferential treatment and racial quotas. Phillip[9] noted that Duke University adopted a five-year plan in 1988 to double the proportion of black faculty, and yet it lost almost as many black faculty as it gained due to attractive job offers elsewhere. Another effort is underway to support and retain as well as to hire minority faculty.

The future of affirmative action remains to be seen. It is clear that many policymakers are rethinking most of the social legislation and commitments made in the last 40-50 years. California legislators are working to modify affirmative action programs. Any change will be exceedingly difficult since so many legislators have built their careers around various advocacy positions for affirmative action. Advocates of rethinking affirmative action point to findings such as those of Joseph Coates, who notes equal access should be replaced by performance criteria. The United States is made up of minorities, and as we face the 21st century there is a clear indication that the Caucasian majority will be a myth since with the rapid influx of minorities from Latin America, South America, China, the present majority will become the minority. Already in some major cities such as San Antonio, Los Angeles and Miami, Hispanics represent the majority. Also, the Caucasian population is made up of many ethnic groups such as the Irish, English, Germans, Scandinavians, etc. It may be that these constituencies will be claiming their affirmative action programs or seeking to abolish those in effect. This may be more urgent if the economy pushes so- called majorities into a jobless, homeless status.

A Current Supreme Court Case

The effort to provide distributive and procedural justice, however, remains a model for western civilization. Throughout the world peoples from less advantaged cultures are attracted to our nation. In American embassies throughout the world, individuals fill waiting rooms to gain entry to the United States. The U.S. green card which grants permission to remain in the country, is a dream for millions. A current Supreme Court Case, *Adarand Constructors Inc. v. Penna 1995,* represented an affirmative action plan being assailed in the Court according to Barrett[10]. The case was brought by Randy Pech, a white Colorado contractor, who installs highway guardrails and claims to have lost business because of racial preferences. Barrett noted that unless a procedural issue sidetracks the Court, there appears to be at least five votes to roll back federal affirmative action: those of Chief Justice William Rehnquist and Justices Antonin Scalia, Clarence Thomas, Anthony Kennedy, and Sandra Day O'Connor. As Barrett reports, the case illustrates the difficult choices facing the administration on affirmative action. On June 12, 1995, Sandra Day O'Connor issuing the court's ruling on a 5 to 4 decision found that federal programs that use race based qualifications must serve a compelling interest and be analyzed under strict scrutiny. Rulings must be narrowly tailored and not broadly interpreted. The impact of this decision may influence educational programs in higher education.

Republicans bolstered by their sweeping November victory are planning to assault affirmative action policies not only in courts (a process underway for several years) but also in Congress and in the states. Some Clinton administration advisors insist that to keep the traditional Democratic base of black and women voters, as well as members of public-employee unions, Mr. Clinton has to fight the antiaffirmative action push. Other advisors contend that Clinton should concede that some affirmative action programs are not effective or fair and need reform.

Meanwhile, it is important to recall, as Chris Lucas[11] points out, that Aristotle held a view that an individual's basic nature and the fortuitous chances of circumstance may play a large role in determining what dispositions are fostered, as well as how they are developed. Because individuals differ in their talents as well as in their social functions within society, the specific form and extent to which good dispositions will be fostered cannot of necessity be the same for all. Yet, as Lucas points out, Aristotle saw education as vital to fill the need to identify what dispositions are to be fostered and how they are to be developed.

The Challenge Remains

One cannot overlook the fact that, as Baida[12] points out, four decades after *Brown v. Board of Education*, racial barriers continue to block equal access to a college education for minority groups still shackled by the painful effects of past discrimination in our country's system of education.

Baida notes that *Podberesky v. Kirwan*, 764 F. Supp. 364 (D. Md. 1991) upheld the constitutionality of a minority scholarship program offered at the University of Maryland, College Park, only to be reversed by the Fourth Circuit, (reversed and remanded, 956 F. 2d 52), 1992; on remand 838 F. Supp. 107 (D. Md. 1993); reversed and remanded, No. 93-2527 (4th Circuit, Oct. 27, 1994). The fourth Circuit Court refused to reconsider the case. The university appealed the case to the Supreme Court which on Monday, May 22, 1995 let the lower court decision stand. This ruling blocks the University of Maryland from granting scholarships based on race.

The University of Maryland created a Benjamin Banneker Scholarship program to increase black enrollment at its main College Park campus.

The scholarship was named after a black scientist who died in 1806. Daniel J. Podberesky, a Hispanic student, brought the lawsuit after he was denied a Banneker scholarship[13]. This case may well be a forerunner of many more to come as *affirmative action* is being rethought in theory and practice. Meanwhile, Baida states that regardless of whether educational institutions are legally required to take corrective action, each has a moral obligation to conduct a critical-self analysis, to ask honestly whether African-Americans and other minority groups receive the same educational opportunities offered to others, and to inquire whether all reasonable steps are being pursued to ensure that this fundamental goal is being achieved.

Another element in university affirmative action programs is the opening of peer review files. While some university administrators feel such a move would be detrimental to hiring the best qualified individuals for a given position, others claim there could be discrimination against women and ethnic minorities if peer review files were closed. Dennis Black, editor of *Perspective*[14], noted that some have argued evaluators must feel free to openly review the work of colleagues, free from the "chilling" effect of possible disclosure. They fear disclosure would result in a less candid and more non-judgmental process. They argue for a process that keeps peer reviews confidential to ensure free exchange of information on colleagues. Black noted that the U.S. Supreme Court in *University of Pennsylvania v. Equal Employment Opportunity Commission* (1990), Justice H. Blackmun speaking for the court, ruled in favor of opening peer review files.

> The costs associated with racial and sexual discrimination in institutions of higher learning are very substantial. Few would deny that ferreting out this kind of invidious discrimination is a great if not compelling governmental interest. Often....disclosure of peer review materials will be necessary...to ...determine whether discrimination has taken place. Indeed, if there is a "smoking gun" to be found that demonstrates discrimination in tenure decision, it is likely to be tucked away in peer review files.

The stage is set for an interesting two years as our reconstituted Congress responds to a perceived mandate of *the less government the better*.

The Expanse of the Language of Affirmative Action

As we face a more litigious society, terms such as *political correctness* and *hostile environment* are surfacing. Affirmative action is being expanded to include environmental perceptions. As Joanne Jacobs[15] notes, universities once places of inquiry and debate, teaching students to challenge old prejudices and to explore new ideas, now are turning to a guaranteed comfort level. Students, she finds, now believe they are entitled to a heavily subsidized education and to an environment and culture sensitive to their unique concerns. These may include single sex computer bulletin boards and lawsuits for a variety of actions and behaviors offending someone's sensitivity. Affirmative action is part and parcel of all educational systems. Colleges and universities universally work to allocate a percentage of their contract business to minority firms. Blumenstyk[16] notes that even if the Court or political leaders move to tighten legal justifications for affirmative action programs in contracting, a number of college officials indicate they will still work to continue these efforts to distribute their funds more broadly. Meanwhile as Blumenstyk points out, the very idea of favoring companies because of the race or sex of their owners offends some people, particularly in cases where no proof of past discrimination has been shown.

Wagner finds[17] that the number of limited-English speakers enrolled in public schools in California has soared 149 percent from 1984 to 1.2 million, a figure that represents about 23 percent of public school students. He notes that Lloyd Chine, affirmative action officer for the San Francisco Unified School District, works to hire additional bilingual teachers who are in great demand. Wagner finds that districts are so desperate for bilingual teachers and competition is so fierce that many use incentives such as stipends, scholarships, and extra help toward getting credentials. With more than 110 different languages being represented in California schools, it is extremely difficult to find available teachers. As Wagner notes, those teachers fluent in Spanish, Cambodian, Vietnamese, Cantonese, Hmong, and Tagalog are almost guaranteed employment in California Schools. He referred to a conservative think tank study by the *Little Hoover Commission,* which found that the state should focus less on teaching children in their own language and more on quickly moving the child into the mainstream with solid English language skills.

Shea[18] reviews a *University of Pennsylvania Law Review* article co-authored by Lani Guinier, which examines women's law school test scores and ranking within class at the end of the first year. The article finds a disproportionate number of women who described law school as a " hostile learning environment" in which women were made to feel intellectually inferior. Women reported the Socratic method of instruction was especially grueling, with one noting that the first year of law school "was like a frightening out-of-body experience". The law review article called for a "reinvention" of legal education. The widening effect of affirmative action continues to be seen in the questions raised about traditional methods of evaluation, instruction, and content in education at all levels and in various degree programs. For some it represents anti-intellectualism with emotions running amok, while others find affirmative action commensurate with democratic theory of responding to individual needs by offering more choices, changing processes, and procedures to expand the nation's commitment to an ever-rising social consciousness enriching the individual and society. Connerly[19] finds that court cases percolate all over the country, but California has staked out political leadership of the drive to take the spoils out of affirmative action on three fronts--at the University of California, in the legislature, and through the initiative process. He notes that the cost of affirmative action is the increasing bitterness of white and Asian-heritage students who find that merit is not enough of what was in the past, an objective process. On the other side, Connerly identifies defenders of quotas who will spare nothing to defend their beachheads at the University of California. Connerly states that the California ferment is partly to reclaim the original rationale for affirmative action which was a way to boost those who needed help in competing on what should be at the point of competition a level playing field. Some current candidates for the Presidency are calling for a colorblind society, with support for equal and unlimited opportunity for all but special privilege for no one[20].

Kit Lively, Yi Shun Lai, Lisa Levenson and Dylan Rivera[21] discussed the University of California Board of Regents' retreat from affirmative action in the *Chronicle of Higher Education*. The Regents' controversial decision entailed achieving diversity without the use of race, ethnicity or gender as a criteria. Jack W. Peltason, president of the California University System, stressed a continued effort to have the system reflect the diverse population of the state.

A Healing Process: A Commitment to the Future

Jacoby[22] calls for a renewed commitment to finding commonalities among people through rediscovering Martin Luther King's call for community and integration, instead of minority enclaves encompassed with mistrust and nastier stereotypes. He finds that mainstream institutions could replace race-conscious remedies with color blind ones-affirmative action programs that target any and all disadvantaged individuals. Jacoby notes that it is time to say no to the tribalistic nonsense that most people now accept as an article of faith---it's a black, white, Jewish, or gay thing and you wouldn't understand. A call for respecting common human values crossing lines of nationalism, cultures and ethnicity, is a starting point to a healing process so essential to finding needed unity out of diversity. President Clinton[23] stressed this healing process recently in his talk at the National Prayer Breakfast. He noted that while words can be the very source of our liberation, possibility, and potential for growth, they can also be used to divide and destroy as never before. Words, he continued, can darken our spirits, weaken our resolve, divide our hearts. We must work together to tear down barriers and do it with greater civility.

While we are working toward civility, we must avoid over-generalization, ad hominem attacks, and diviseness which often leads to making our schools and colleges battlegrounds for competing ideologies and single interest causes. Extraordinary and extreme sensitivity to language usage, if not examined and critiqued, may lead to educators who are afraid to utter a statement not acceptable to each separate interest group. Isolationism as reflected in California's Proposition 187 is not an appropriate response to the needs of the 21st century. Censorship, status quo, appeal to crowd psychology, and 'us against them' philosophy will diminish the role of education in an open democratic society. Respect for varying viewpoints, differing perceptions, diverse cultures and peoples, attitudes and beliefs is the mortar that binds a civilized society.

As educators we are encouraged to predict future trends. One may with some degree of risk because of unforeseen events such as *systems breaks* state that outside of minor adjustments, *affirmative action programs and commitments* may not change much as we approach the 21st century. The rationale for this prediction is that both the advocates and the opponents of the issue have generated strong support for their positions. One may also predict that affirmative action may neither be expanded in the future nor weakened. The one factor that may change this prediction is an excessiveness of government regulations. These regulations greatly increase the cost of business and industry in the United States as is true in all other institutions within society. Thus there is a move for rethinking affirmative action by leaders in Congress. Harlan Cleveland[24] notes that finding ways to become unified despite diversity may be the world's most pressing problem in the years ahead.

References:

1. Rawls, John (1971). *A Theory of Justice,* Cambridge, MS: Harvard University Press, 430, 428.
2. Judge, Janet; O'Brien, David; O'Brien, Timothy (1995). "Gender Equity in the 1990's: An Athletic Administrators Survival Guide to Title IX and Gender Equity Compliance," *Seton Hall Journal of Sports Law.*
3. Rawls, John, *Ibid:* 302-303.
4. Pulliam, John, and Van Patten, James (1995). *History of Education in America,* Prentice-Hall: 258.
5. Frank, Robert and De Lisser, Eleena (1995). "Research on Affirmative Action Finds Modest Gaines for Blacks Over 30 Years", *Wall Street Journal,* Feb. 21, 1995: A2, A8.
6. Julnes, Ralph E. (1994). "OCR and the Affirmative Action Controversy: An Explanation", *West's Education Law Quarterly;* April, v 3, n2: 338-50.
7. Opp, Ronald D. (1994). "Minority versus White Administrators' Perceptions of the Recruitment and Retention of Minority Faculty in Two Year Colleges", *Journal of Applied Research in the Community College,* V1, n 2,:85-99.
8. Rodriguez, Roberto (1994). "Higher Education Crisis Looms for Chicanos/Latinos", *Black Issues in Higher Education,* April, V11, n3: 30-23.
9. Phillip, Mary Christine (1994). "Affirmative Action Still Saddled with Negative Image: Bad Mouthing by Beneficiaries Baffles Many", *Black Issues in Higher Education,* V11, n2:24-26.
10. Barrett, Paul M. (1994). "Affirmative-Action Plan is Assailed in the Supreme Court", *Wall Street Journal,* Wednesday, January 18, 1995: B6.
11. Lucas, Christopher J. (1972). *Our Western Educational Heritage,* New York: Macmillan: 90.
12. Baida, Andrew H. (1994). "Not All Minority Scholarships Are Created Equal", *The Journal of College and University Law,* Volume 21, n4: 307,352

13. Moore, Arden (May 1995). "Education Officials Unsure About Effects of Court Ruling", *Sun Sentinel (Palm Beach County, Florida)*, Tuesday, P. 8A.
14. Black, Dennis R. (May 1990). "Supreme Court Opens Peer Review Files", Editor, *Perspective*:1.
15. Jacobs, Joanne, (1994). " Hostile Environment Idea Ravaging Academia", *Tulsa World*, Friday, October 7, News 13.
16. Blumenstyk, Goldie (1995). "Battle Over 'Set-Asides", *The Chronicle of Higher Education*, February 10: A27-28.
17. Wagner, Venise, (1994). "Schools Vie for Bilingual Teachers", *San Francisco Examiner*, Sunday, February 5, C-1.
18. Shea, Christopher (1995). "Ginier says 'Insidious' Sexism Mars Legal Education for Women", *The Chronicle of Higher Education"*, February 10: A25.
19. Connerly, Ward (1995). "Affirmative Action", *Wall Street Journal*, Feb. 20, 1995: A24.
20. "Top Republican Candidates Seek to Eliminate Affirmative Action". (Monday, February 20, 1995). *Tulsa World*: 5.
21. Lively, Kit, Lai, Yi Shun, Levenson, Lisa and Rivera, Dylan (August 4, 1995). *The Chronicle of Higher Education:*A 18.
22. Jacoby, Tamar, (1994). "An Integrationist Manifesto", *Wall Street Journal*, Tuesday, October 4, 1994: A18.
23. Clinton, Bill (1995). "A President Calls for Words that Heal, Not Hurt", Excerpts from remarks made Feb. 2 at the National Prayer Breakfast, Washington, D.C., *Christian Science Monitor*, Friday, February 17:19.
24. Cleveland, Harlan (1995). "The Limits to Cultural Diversity", *The Futurist*, March-April:23-26.

Chapter 6

Academic Freedom and Tenure

Frederick Eby[1] identifies the origins of Western higher education. Religious temples were centers of advanced learning in Egypt. Heliopolis (City of the Sun), according to Eby, was a popular center of learning. Moses, Thales, and Plato studied in Egypt. Other temples were centers of learning with stress on subjects such as medical and military education and the priesthood. Athens and Rome served as centers of learning. As Eby states, the university is a product of the Middle Ages. Its character was established in the 12th and 13th centuries. Among the earliest universities were Bologna, Paris, and Oxford. They flourished due in part to the unity in Western Europe under the Pope, respect for knowledge, and the development of a body of scholars in Western Europe. Instructors were often clergy who attracted young people with their bright and shining light of criticism of authority. Criticism of church dogma, however, often led to untimely demise of instructors. Peter Abelard was put out of action due not only to his teaching but his amorous relationships with a nun. Challenge to the status quo was not tolerated.

Instructors were peripatetic teachers wandering from place to place attracting students. With no fixed facilities, students and faculty could move easily from one community to another. If townspeople raised rents, it was easy to move. Societies of guilds by masters and students were formed to give universities a corporate character. Bologna became a center for revival of Roman law. It was here that law was established as a subject of professional study. The University of Paris became a model for Oxford. Early college catalogues indicated that the curriculum and rites of passage would model the University of Paris. Later Harvard College was founded on the manner of Oxford. With few books, lectures, repetition, disputation and examination predominated, with rote memorization and rhetoric utilized as teaching methods. The University of Paris in 1215 provided through statute that students read the whole of Aristotle's logical works.

Students formed guilds issuing so many decrees for instructors to follow that instructors themselves formed guilds to get back at students who insisted on a bond if an instructor had to leave town for any reason. An instructor with less than five students was fined. Students required them to begin with the bell and quit within one minute of a bell. Since professors depended on student fees, they were restricted. Guilds of masters soon corrected the situation by requiring students to take certain classes guaranteeing an adequate enrollment in order to gain a license to teach anywhere in Christendom.

Curriculum included the trivium and quadrivium making up the seven liberal arts. Grammar, Rhetoric, and Logic were to be combined with Arithmetic, Geometry, Astronomy and Music. The European universities provided the model for Harvard College and those that followed in Colonial New England.

Instructors taught truth as revealed by authority and were generally faithful to authoritarian dogma. Those who failed to adhere to accepted Church Dogma were subject to the inquisition or ostracized. St. Anselm's statement "I believe in order that I may know" provided the philosophy of education for the period.

Autonomy

Eby reports that a great riot of 1228-1229 resulted in soldiers killing some students. The masters suspended lectures in support of students and when this failed to bring redress closed the university for a period of six years. Pope Gregory IX intervened in the quarrel, punished the offenders against the university, and issued a "papal bull" giving his sanctions to certain privileges of the universities. In 1245, Pope Innocent IV granted scholars of the University of Paris exemption from appearing in ecclesiastical courts at a distance from Paris, and the following year instituted a Court of Conservation whose duty was to protect the university. In time, the faculty and university achieved status that made it independent of local, civil, and ecclesiastical officials[2]. University autonomy provided special privileges to scholars and masters and is still represented in various ways in the modern world. Over time and with the help of the German experience in developing academic freedom, American universities followed suit. Research and scholarship were essential to suspended judgment and changing truth that reflected rigor in scholarship. German university concepts of academic freedom meant *lernfreiheit and lehrfreiheit*. *Lernfreiheit* or freedom of the university student to choose courses, move from school to school, and be free from dogmatic restrictions eventually was adopted by American research universities. *Lehrfreiheit* provided for the right of the university professor to freedom of inquiry and freedom of teaching with the right to study and report on findings in an unhindered, unrestricted and unfettered environment[3]. Current attempts to legislate productivity and accountability interfere with the central purpose of higher education. These attempts interfere with an ideal of university autonomy. Although academic freedom is threatened on many fronts, the value of the concept is clearly stated in *Sweezy v. New Hampshire* (1957):

The essentiality of freedom in the community of American universities is almost self-evident. No one should underestimate the vital role in a democracy that is played by those who guide and train our youth. To impose any straitjacket upon the intellectual leaders in our colleges and universities would imperil the future of our nation. No field of education is so thoroughly comprehended by man that new discoveries cannot yet be made. Particularly is that true in the social sciences, where few, if any, principles are accepted as absolutes. Scholarship cannot flourish in an atmosphere of suspicion and distrust. Teachers and students must always remain free to inquire, to study, and to evaluate, to gain new maturity and understanding; otherwise, our civilization will stagnate and die (354 U.S. at 250).

Recently there has been legal and state legislature concern about overly broad interpretations of academic freedom in the realm of free speech. However, the value of academic freedom to a democracy continues to be recognized regardless of the vagrancies of political perspectives. Faculty members' academic freedom within their areas of competence and expertise should remain unhindered.

Tenure

In 1915 the *American Association of University Professors* was established. Scholars such as John Dewey had been receiving letters from faculty members throughout the country relating incidents of dismissal because of bias and political pressure. A corporation president might send a letter to a university president informing him of a faculty member who was rumored to be against the free enterprise system or capitalism. The industrial titan would seek the instructor's dismissal. Many states had provisions for dismissing faculty at will. To protect faculty members from capricious anti-intellectual attacks tenure or job protection was increasingly supported. Tenure is granted after a probationary period which varies in duration from institution to institution. Often mentors assist new professors in adjusting to the academic world. After a probationary period, the professor is assured job continuance if performance continues satisfactory. Grounds for dismissal are moral turpitude, incompetence, and criminal activity. In recent years with more strident demands for accountability, tenured faculty are reviewed yearly to assure they are keeping up with their field and maintaining an acceptable level of productivity. Legislatures and the public are examining and rethinking tenure, questioning whether it has anything to do with academic freedom or if tenure is just a route to job security.

With a more litigious society, individuals who are denied tenure may take their cases to court. Leatherman[4] reports on a case at Vassar College. A tenured biologist, who was not involved in a departmental denial of tenure to a female faculty member, had his academic record reviewed by a court. The review was undertaken to determine if tenured faculty members had a record of productivity equal to, less than or better than, individuals denied tenure. The woman claimed her work was equal to if not better than that of other members of the department and brought a sex discrimination lawsuit. The judge ordered her reinstatement with tenure. Leatherman finds that turning the spotlight on credentials of colleagues has become a popular legal strategy for faculty who are denied tenure. Denial of tenure after the probationary period usually means termination which is set forth in the initial contract of employment.

In sex discrimination cases, the appealing party seeks to go after the full professor with tenure who has the weakest publication record. Often court judges may not understand a faculty member's contribution to scholarship or may belittle his achievements. When an individual's record is investigated and widely disseminated, Leatherman reports there is often humiliation and loss of prestige. In some cases the innocent bystander leaves the profession rather than face a hostile working environment.

Douglas Lederman and Carolyn J. Mooney[5] in *Lifting the Cloak of Secrecy from Tenure* discussed the lifting of the veil of secrecy from tenure decision making at Ohio's public colleges. The Ohio Supreme Court in August of 1994 ruled that tenure files should be opened. After reviewing the files at Ohio State University, Lederman and Mooney found that in almost every negative tenure case, inadequate research was the major reason cited. In most public higher education institutions, tenure review is undertaken from four to seven years after the initial hiring date. Research, advising, teaching and service are generally reviewed but as Lederman and Mooney noted politics, race and money can influence a tenure case and there are occasionally cases of departments split over personalities or politics.

The race for tenure among junior faculty members puts physical and emotional pressure on them and their families as they frequently burn the midnight oil to publish, acquire grants and engage in research. Acquisition of tenure, however, is not the nirvana many expect. Most higher education institutions require yearly evaluations of tenured faculty and a high level of productivity is expected.

Lederman[6] also explores the challenge of diversity goals and the tenure process. College administrators may challenge tenure panel recommendations on the basis of the special dimension of professional contributions to cultural and ethnic diversity. There are no easy answers to responding to the need for representation of diverse populations within the higher education faculty. He cited an Ohio State case in which an administrator noted that it was entirely appropriate to create a position for a minority candidate and go to "unusual lengths"---including extra research support and teaching load reductions---to help a candidate succeed. The chapter on affirmative action explores this issue further.

The historical rationale for tenure as a protection for academic freedom remains viable as we approach the 21st century. Faculty needs the protection tenure provides to disseminate research regardless of how innovative, creative or proactive or at odds with current knowledge it may be. For centuries it was not acceptable to profess that the world was round. Existing knowledge excluded such a position. Today as in the past, faculty needs to be free to engage in dialogue, inquiry and discovery without fear of being silenced.

References:

1.   Eby, Frederick (1940). *The History and Philosophy of Education: Ancient and Medieval.* New York: Prentice-Hall: 95, 785-788, 756-761.
2.   Ibid:780.
3.   Rudolph, Frederick (1962). *The American College and University,* New York: Random House, Vintage Books: 412.
4.   Leatherman, Courtney (1995). "Credentials on Trial", *The Chronicle of Higher Education,* February 3: A-14-A16.
5.   Lederman, Douglas and Mooney, Carolyn J. (April 14, 1995). " Lifting the Cloak of Secrecy from Tenure", *The Chronicle of Higher Education.*
6.   Lederman, Douglas (April 14, 1995). "Wrestling With the Issue of Race", *The Chronicle of Higher Education.*

Chapter 7

Future Trends and Issues in Higher Education

Educational institutions like others are essentially political in nature. Decisions are often made on the basis of a compromise between competing groups and interest sectors seeking the larger share of a smaller fiscal pie. As we approach the 21st century, there will be an increased demand for more effective, responsive and timely delivery systems. Universities and colleges can no longer do business as usual. Systematic efforts should be made, however, to assure a positive, healthy, organizational climate. The morale of individuals within institutions is an important factor in maintaining a good quality of life for all its various populaces. Regardless of external and internal pressures to increase productivity, accountability and performance, organizational stewards need to be ever vigilante in supporting the humane use of human beings. Legislators, parents, students, professional higher education organizations and the public facing increased taxes, all are seeking more accountability and professionalism from faculty. Students are demanding more from their college experience since many are working full time, placebound students, or non-traditional students, who are seeking better instruction on a more cost effective basis. Some experimental three year baccalaureate degree programs are currently being implemented. These programs are designed to limit the tuition costs of undergraduate students as well as to explore innovative curricular models that question the traditional requisite of some 120 plus hours for a baccalaureate degree.

Colleges and universities are employing an increased variety of marketing techniques for student recruitment. Offering guarantees of four-year graduation is more common. If a student is unable to get a class, he or she needs, of if there is misadvisement, some colleges will pay for a fifth year of matriculation. College administrators are accepting the responsibility to see students graduate on time. With a declining pool of college bound youth, marketing is gaining a foothold in higher education[1]. An additional recruitment technique is substance-free housing. Smoke, and drug free dorms are becoming more common. The trend is still in its infancy, but university administrators and student associations are getting involved in the programs. The idea may or may not have long term significance, but it does indicate the ways college leaders are working to appeal to a variety of student concerns[2].

Faculty members are pressured by mixed signals to publish more, to acquire more grants, and to teach more effectively. Many are stretched very thin and work a 60-80 hour week to keep up with student and publishing demands. While an almost universal message to instructors now is the importance of effective teaching and the sanctity of student evaluations, bottom line promotions and rewards most often go to those who have published most or acquired major grants. Faculty members will need to be more adept at playing the workload game. With a focus on accountability, many departmental, college, and university regulations stipulate breaking down time spent on various tasks into percentages. Thus, for example an individual faculty member may be required to identify the percentage of time spent on advising, teaching, research and service.

Individuals need to become acquainted with the statistical analysis that may not reward outstanding performance in a low percentage area. As John Dewey[3] noted in his *Individualism Old and New,* quantification, mechanization and standardization are the marks of Americanization that is conquering the world. Love of the adventure of learning, a quest for creativity, an unhindered search for new knowledge may be handicapped by the restricted environment of reductionism. Although there are some current efforts to provide more flexibility in the reward system, the ranking and rating game prevails. Faculty members also need to be alert to changing funding formulas. They may be switched from stress on productivity as measured by retention, recruitment and graduation of a diverse student population to focus on enrollment figures. The change depends on legislative perceptions of the most effective utilization of resources and social priorities.

Academic freedom and tenure will be increasingly scrutinized by legislators as they question the need for both. Historians of higher education may see in this movement a return to the anti-intellectualism of the past.

None of us can predict the future with certainty, but it appears the age of information and technology will increasingly affect higher education. Internet communication will bring scholars closer so that those in similar academic areas can share their interest and expertise. This will enhance global understanding, respect for other cultures and recognition that we need to communicate on the superinformation highway.

With no age limit to working years, there will be concern about higher health care and employment costs. Studies to date have indicated there will not be a problem with senior employees staying beyond the period of their effectiveness. In most instances, those who remain beyond traditional employment years are highly productive and David Boren, President of the University of Oklahoma is exploring the use of senior faculty to teach part time in the undergraduate division.

Higher education institutions will reflect the mood of the larger social order, as administrators increasingly yield to legislative decrees. There will be more restrictions emerging on all of the traditional forms of academic ritual and trappings. As higher education institutions seek to become nationally recognized research 1 institutions, they will continue to raise student tuition costs. In addition, many universities decision makers will look to foreign students who pay full out of state tuition costs to help carry the load of an increasing number of needy students.

New faculty members in major research universities will increasingly be denied tenure for failure to publish. Depending on the university, the quality or quantity of the publications will be the basis for awarding tenure. With a limited number of professional journals, competition for publication will increase. A variety of creative ways of getting published will emerge including internet electronic journals, desk top publishing, creating special periodicals for faculty manuscripts and self publishing efforts.

Under emerging changes in funding for universities, retention of minority faculty and students as well as graduation rates may be the criteria for funding. These productivity formulas may replace student full time equivalent head count as a funding method. How long this emerging trend will continue is hard to predict. State legislators may rethink these funding formulas especially if enrollment declines excessively or standards are raised so high many state high school graduates will not be able to enter the university of their choice. This is a continuing issue-- how to balance higher standards with the need for a state's students to have access to colleges and universities. Higher education administrators are adaptable to changing demographics and enrollment trends. When there is a decline in traditional student enrollment, recruitment of non-traditional students is implemented to take up the slack. If higher student standards lead to a decline in enrollment, they are modified to maintain the organization's enrollment. When enrollment is increasing, college and university administrators raise standards. Higher education institutions are increasingly market oriented and administrators adjust to varying economic and political influences.

A companion issue is the current trend to analyze student development programs designed to help students at risk through college remedial programs. Many legislators are questioning the cost of remedial courses in higher education and some are in favor of abolishing them entirely. This is a hard call since many students excel in their studies after completing remedial courses. Perhaps there will be more attention to assisting high schools in their preparation of students. More work in the field of motivation will be helpful in the future as the nation works to upgrade students' academic credentials. Students who have English as a second language, recent arrivals to our country, require additional work to matriculate successfully in higher education.

Community colleges will continue to be feeder systems for colleges and will serve to meet remedial education requirements. They will improve articulation agreements with universities so they can more adequately prepare their students for junior and senior level work. Community colleges will continue to strengthen their linkages to high schools in order to assure adequate and relevant student preparation for higher education.

The cost of higher education will continue to increase as inflation takes its toll. We must be careful not to price worthy students out of the market. Most major universities maintain fund raising departments on a full time basis. These foundation funds provide for a margin of excellence but it will be increasingly difficult to raise more money as higher education institutions seek to tap the largess from corporate America.

Our nation has an economic system which fluctuates between boom and bust. We have never been able to smooth out the downcycles, so higher education institutions will always be faced with periods requiring retrenchment, reallocation of resources and recycling faculty from academic programs with less longterm promise to those of rapid growth. A final challenge to higher education institutions is the increasingly litigious society. Lawsuits are common in our colleges and universities and take a larger amount of time and funds that would normally go into the instructional effort.

Our higher education institutions have provided opportunities to generations of students who have enriched our society. We have a pluralistic, open, democratic society whose institutions provide opportunities for all its citizens. There is a college or university that will meet the needs of all individuals who seek higher education. Opportunities exist for students with varying academic records and potential as well as those with varying interests and needs. The strength of our higher education systems is reflected in the increasing multiculturalism and diversity of students. In addition there are an increasing number of foreign students who come to the United States for college degrees. Foreign students often comprise a majority of the students in graduate programs in engineering and the pure sciences.

Although tuition costs continue to increase, the expenses for a degree are still below those in many other countries. The future for higher education will be challenging and filled with opportunities to implement new delivery systems and reach a larger student body. Internet outreach programs are being utilized to reach an off campus student body, and new nontraditional outreach programs through distance learning are serving students throughout the nation. These new alternative delivery systems reflect what Alvin Toffler referred to as "Third Wave" paradigms that empower individuals and organizations to better fulfill goals and missions.

We must be vigilant to avoid imposing management systems foreign to the **Ideal of the University**, on higher education systems. Good management of university resources can be done effectively without the imposition of business and industry micromanagement ideology inappropriate for people centered learning centers where the search for knowledge and truth occurs most effectively in an environment unhindered by the fetters which would restrain and limit creativity.

This exploration of the culture of higher education, its weaknesses and strengths, is clarified by Brubacher[4] in his *On the Philosophy of Higher Education:*

The university is the most honorable and the least corrupt institution in American life. It is, with the church, the one institution that has, through all our history, served or tried to serve the interests of the whole of mankind and the interests of truth. No other institution can perform the functions which the university performs, no other can fill the place which it has long filled and with such intelligence and moral influence.

This book would be incomplete if I did not express appreciation for a scholar, mentor and model for my professional career. Chancellor Emeritus William Pearson Tolley of Syracuse University never wavered from his firm commitment to the freedoms so essential for learning and teaching. He wrote:

Education should deal with the whole [person]....Schools and colleges should minister as best they can to the needs of the whole [person]. They should try to inculcate integrity and honor. They should try to build character. They should attempt to protect our health. They should attempt to keep us sensitive to religious and moral values. They should try to give us concern for beauty as well as truth and goodness. And finally, they are conscious of the unmet needs of the world. They should try to teach us to be good citizens and to be socially useful (5:103).

References:

1.   Spaid, Elizabeth Levitan (August 28, 1995). "Colleges Step Up Marketing Efforts", *Christian Science Monitor:* 13.
2.   Belsie, Laurent (August 30, 1995). "Temperance Movement Hits College Dorms", *Christian Science Monitor:* 1,18.
3.   Dewey, John (1930). *Individualism Old and New.* New York: Capricorn Books: 24.
4.   Brubacher, John (1982). *On The Philosophy of Higher Education.* San Francisco, Jossey Bass: 135.
5.   Tolley, William Pearson (1977). *The Adventure of Learning.* Syracuse: Syracuse University Press: 103

Case Studies Listing

List of Selected Authors

Reference is to the first occurance of the name of the Selected Author.

Definition of Terms

Academic Freedom- freedom to teach without fear of interference from the public or from those who are opposed to listening to all points of view.

Affirmative Action-governmental guidelines for enhancing access to education and employment for minorities, women, and mentally and physically challenged.

Autonomy-higher education institutional freedom from outside interference (church, state) with teaching, learning process and search for new knowledge and truth.

Downsize-eliminating faculty, or programs when there is a funding reduction.

Hardening of the Categories-so stuck in a status quo belief system that one does not listen to or respect the ideas of others if they are different from one's own.

Incentive Funding-provision for additional state funding for higher education institutions that increase graduate and retention rates as well as increase minority student, faculty, administration population.

Full Time Equivalent-identifying full time student categories.

Leadership Styles-*Exploitative/Authoritative or Benevolent/Authoritative* leadership tends to result in organizations characterized by threats, fear, punishment, top-down communication, and centralized decisionmaking and control. The stress is on subordinate conformity to organizational goals and productivity standards. *Consultative/Participative (Democratic)* leadership tends to result in an organization that evidences trust, collaborative goal setting, bottom-up communication and supportive leadership behavior. (Razik, Taher, A. and Swanson, Austin D. (1995) *Fundamental Concepts of Educational Leadership and Management.* Columbus, Ohio, Merrill. "Likert's Four Leadership Styles" p. 43. There are many variations on these leadership styles as well as new efforts to understand leadership within a cultural and organizational transformational context.

Lernfreiheit- freedom of the university student to chose courses, move from school to school and be free from dogmatic restrictions.

Lehrfreiheit-right of the university professor to freedom of inquiry and teaching. Right to study and report on findings in an unhindered, unrestricted, and unfettered environment in one's area of expertise.

Micromanagement-excessive supervision of faculty which diminishes opportunity for faculty creativity and innovation in their areas of expertise.

Peer Review-retention, promotion based on performance review by peers in similar academic disciplines in other institutions. Faculty books and articles submitted for publication are reviewed by peers in a professional field. Articles are often chosen for publication on the basis of peer review.

Placebound-students who have high earning power, families and are unable to take time off to engage in traditional degree studies and programs.

Programmatic Justification-providing rationale for eliminating low producing or increasing high potential programs within higher education.

Sabbatical-faculty paid leaves given after a period of service to an institution of higher education. Provides faculty an opportunity for academic renewal, publication and networking with colleagues in fields of expertise. Sabbaticals encourage interchange of ideas and research among and between faculty within and outside an institution.

Systems Breaks-unexpected events, happenings, occurrences that may change projections as to student enrollment, tenure and organizational growth. Financial exigency is an example of a systems break. An unexpected financial shortfall may lead to reduction in staff and reallocation of resources.

Tenure-provision for job security to allow publication and teaching of one's field of expertise. It protects individuals from anti-intellectual attacks.

Index

References are to page numbers. Names of Case Studies are not included, they are shown on page 85. Names of Selected authors are not included, they are listed on page 87. Definition of terms are not included, they are shown on page 89.